THE FAITH PRINCIPLES

"Faith That Works"

by Valkeith Ulysses Williams

THE FAITH PRINCIPLES:
"FAITH THAT WORKS"

Printed in the United States of America

First Printing 2018

ISBN: 978-0-692-97465-0

Future N vestment
2291 Raleigh Court
Clarksville, TN 37043

ABOUT THE COVER

The Grand Canyon with a tightrope stretched from one side to the other, with a man standing on one end preparing to walk across.

The man has options: a parachute, a safety net, or a rope. But, within this cover, you do not see any of the options in place. Why? The man will attempt to cross in faith. He will not consider his own abilities, but his trust in God. *"Now faith is the substance of things hoped for, the evidence of things not seen" Hebrew 11:1 (KJV).*

He has attempted and achieved great feats similar to this in the past, but this attempt is somewhat different. When it comes to crossing the Grand Canyon, there is a bit of a challenge due to the winds produced in the hollow of the canyon. The man will meet and exceed his normal accomplishments somewhere in the proximity of 1200 feet from either side and 1500 feet above ground, but it is only when he is in the middle of the canyon, the effects of the winds on the rope create the greatest challenge; affecting the stability of the rope, which now challenges the man's ability to balance. *"'Yes, come,' Jesus said. So Peter went over the side of the boat and walked on the water toward Jesus. But when he saw the strong wind and the waves, he was terrified and began to sink. 'Save me, Lord!'*

he shouted. Jesus immediately reached out and grabbed him. 'You

have so little faith,' Jesus said. 'Why did you doubt me?'" Matthew

14:29-31 (NLT).

In the scenario on the cover, everything is a constant, meaning they

do not change, except the one thing you do not see. And that is the

wind! But, the man's faith should not change because the wind

changes! He shouldn't vacillate in his faith due to what he already

knows can happen. It is the same with your faith, as you operate in

the unknown and unseen way of life; nonetheless, believing you will

always be victorious! As for the man, getting to the other side should

be similar to that of strolling down a sidewalk, which is very wide

and safe, having no fear of what is to his left and right. Let's call his

trip a sidewalk journey in faith.

DEDICATION

Dedication is to commit to a goal, a way of life or to inscribe or address by way of compliment--Merriam-Webster.com.

Well, I have accomplished the first part of the definition: committed to a goal by completing this book. But, the second part of the definition goes far beyond *"me!"* Therefore, I would like to dedicate this book to my Lord and Savior Jesus Christ, who is "the author and finisher of our faith" *Hebrews 12:2 (KJV)*. Therefore, I want to compliment Him for all He has done, is doing, and will do in my life. Because He has given me so much: a life and an abundant life. Families, both biological and spiritual! He has saved me eternally and so many times from earthly death. This is so important because the devil has tried so many times to abort God's plan for my life. Satan knew I had the potential for writing this book; therefore he tried to keep it from coming forth. But, God! Jesus sacrificed His life for me so I would be able to write this book and present it to you. My Lord, I thank you for thinking about little ole' me. Who am I? I am a person operating in greatness when operating under Your power and authority! Who am I in the grand scheme of things? I am mighty when conquering in Your strength! Therefore, You are worthy to be praised! Who am I? I am the one who *loves* You for making me great and mighty— *"Loving God means keeping his commandments, and his commandments are not burdensome" 1 John 5:3 (NLT)*. So, I ask You to send the rain! Why? Because there has been a drought in the land. Now open the floodgates of heaven for *Your people*! Amen.

ACKNOWLEDGEMENTS

First, I would like to acknowledge God for allowing me to reach this pinnacle in my life and for giving His son Jesus Christ for the redemption of my sins. Who spoke to me through the Spirit, to write and complete this book! He said, "I will make it great and prosperous; now write!"

Secondly, I would like to acknowledge my family, especially my wife "BJ" for hanging in there, with patience while I procrastinated and prolonged this longer than expected. Nevertheless, holding on while I went through the process of achieving this great feat. I love you! And to our children: Kiebe (daughter), DeVal (son), and Bralix (grandson and *graphics & cover designer)*, who are a part of our destiny and vice versa. I love you!

Thirdly, I would like to acknowledge the past and present saints of Ekklesia Christian Church International, Inc. who unknowingly caused me to birth this book into existence. Leaving a legacy and an inheritance are so key in a father's life. God is your Father! I am ONLY His representative in the earth! But, as some of you have grown up and gone your separate ways, I know in my heart I am still that *father in the faith* figure to you. I would like to give a special thanks to my dear Spiritual Leaders in the faith, whether superiors, peers, or subordinates for your mentorship, guidance, and unknowingly deposits of spiritual nuggets in my life, which represented nutrients during the process of carrying and birthing this phenomenal book. I have learned to stay teachable, therefore you all had something to give and it was much appreciated. A special thanks to Dr. Curtis Glenn, Divine Creation Ministries who was willing to share, mentor, and cast vision in the birth of this baby (i.e., book). It was not easy, but God was relentless in His efforts to get this baby (i.e., book) to you. *Now, grow it (share it with others); then, let it grow you, by taking in what it has for you by giving yourself to it!!* Thanks to all!

TABLE OF CONTENTS

PREFACE

The Bible reveals, *"faith without works is dead."* It also reveals, *"Now faith is the substance of things hoped for the evidence of things not seen." Hebrews. 11:1 (KJV)*

The objective of this book is NOT to take away from the Bible, but present "Faith" in a way you can apply the "Faith Principles," and have fun doing so. You know when coaches or trainers apply various methods to making exercising fun and people get excited about working out to the point it becomes a routine part of their everyday. This book should give you that same type gym experience, by exercising your faith, where trusting and believing in the power of God becomes a routine part of your day. In doing so, God will be glorified and you will reap the benefits! You might be thinking, "What benefits?" The benefits of an abundant life! This book was written using men in the Bible who operated in faith, challengingly it was also written to title their "faith" for the purpose of providing you nuggets to add to your future "FAITH BAG."

This book is short in length and breviloquent: use of very few words (i.e., concise), but powerful in content! Many of the "Faith Principles" described were applicable to men in the Bible and their life experiences, which are now lifelong testimonies documented as a historical records in the Bible. Please, do not let the testimonies *alone* be your motivation to try God's "Faith Principles!" Allow *faith **in*** God to be your motivating factor.

Childlike "FAITH" is a great example of trusting when there is nothing left to do but trust! *"But Jesus said, 'Let the children come to me. Don't stop them! For the Kingdom of Heaven belongs to those who are like these children'" Matthew 19:14 (NLT).* Think about a child, or even when you were a child, the trust you had that Dad or Mom would catch you when you purposefully decided to let go of the table, chair, or couch and attempted to walk over to him/her. And once you did it, you were cracking smiles and laughing with excitement. Dad and/or Mom were just as excited. Wow! Now, can you visualize it today, you bursting out in laughter and jumping for joy at the experience of God being faithful in response to your faith, giving you that confidence that He would catch you! And can you visualize how excited He will be knowing you trust Him? Now you have a glimpse of why people run and jump for joy in church. You may not be there yet, but one day you will. Do you want change in your life? Then, you need to try *"faith that works!"* Previously, it was mentioned the "gym experience." Well, many gyms offer awesome protein shakes to replenish gym-goers as part of their gym experience. And I think if you were to try one of these *"faith that works"* shakes; you will surely be replenished. Just funning with you! You may ask, what is it and how does it really work? Do not fret, because each segment contains explanations and supporting scriptures to build your faith. Pay special attention to EACH PRINCIPLE and take out your "FAITH BAG," so you can fill it with God's special nuggets!

What is a principle? Merriam-Webster.com defines a "principle" as

1. A moral rule or belief that helps you know what is right and wrong and that influences your actions

2. Basic truth or theory: an idea that forms the basis of something

3. A law or fact of nature that explains how something works or why something happens

Now, you can begin your journey toward applying "faith" in accordance with the aforementioned definitions and the *faith principles* forthcoming. Therefore, "faith principle" would be defined as,

1. Word of God: that helps you know what is right and wrong and that influences your actions

2. Truth from God: that forms the basis of your belief and faith

3. Facts from God: that explains how faith works or why supernatural things happen

Since "faith principle" has been defined and narrowed in its meaning, now turn your attention to applying it to your daily life.

In the next seven segments, allow God to open your eyes, not just to the meaning and results of faith; but to the ***principle behind*** the faith or principle applied to the faith action. Our beloved Peter in the Bible had faith, but to see it (yes you can *see* faith) he had to step off the boat to activate it! So, what belief, truth, or fact did he possess that ***caused*** him to take that first step? After reading this book you should take possession of the same cause and effect that Peter used to "*walk on water*." For the record, I am not telling you to try walking on water, but trust God enough to receive ***that*** breakthrough you have always wanted in life!

Are you ready for this journey?

ENJOY!

SEGMENT I

NEHEMIAH'S FAITH
"52 Days Principle"

Why did God reveal such a name for this faith? Why such a principle? Well, He wanted to explain that Nehemiah *prepared* for building the wall of Jerusalem, but it ONLY took him and the people 52 days to build it. *"So on October 2 the wall was finished—just fifty-two days after we had begun" Nehemiah 6:15 (NLT)*. The faith principle God wants to highlight is in 52 days of starting a project *in faith* and *not coming off the wall*, you too can accomplish your goal(s).

Remember, this was a wall around an entire city! There were some distractions, but Nehemiah did not stop the *great work* that he had set out to accomplish. *"But when Sanballat and Tobiah and the Arabs, Ammonites, and Ashdodites heard that the work was going ahead and that the gaps in the wall of Jerusalem were being repaired, they were furious" Nehemiah 4:7 (NLT)*. You too will have Sanballat, Tobiah, and Geshem the Arab as distractions against completing a *great work* in your life!

How many projects have you attempted, but stopped or you did not obtain the results you wanted? How many New Year resolutions have you set, but never completed? Could it be that the distractions, the procrastination, the lack of discipline, or any other excuse has hindered, blocked, or kept you from achieving your goal? Good news, *you still can finish*! And you will learn how too as you continue reading this book.

The start of the finished work/project goes something like this: Nehemiah was a servant to a king, but to be in the place where the king's kingdom resided, Nehemiah had to come from somewhere. Please note, Nehemiah's homeland was not where he worked; it was in **Judah**. And while Nehemiah was displaced from his homeland something tragic occurred: *"the city where my ancestors are buried is in ruins, and the gates have been destroyed by fire," Nehemiah 2:3 (NLT)* and when Nehemiah learned of the event it truly disturbed and troubled him to a point the king recognized his servant's performance had decreased and his expression was that of gloom. *"I had never before appeared sad in his presence. So the king asked* *me, "Why are you looking so sad? You don't look sick to me. You must be deeply troubled," Nehemiah 2:1-2 (NLT).*

Do you have a job that has you displaced from your homeland, hometown or place you desire to live? Are events happening back home with your family, friends, loved ones that have you troubled or disturbed? Does your boss see a difference in your performance due to what is happening in your life? Does your boss really care? Well, he should, because what is affecting you will eventually affect him.

Nehemiah's boss was concerned about his servant. And rightfully so, Nehemiah was the cupbearer and in his condition he could have easily overlooked tasting or inspecting the wine, which could have been given to the king, causing great sickness or even his death. *"The king asked, 'Well, how can I help you?' With a prayer to the God of heaven, I replied, 'If it please the king, and if you are pleased with me, your servant, send me to Judah to rebuild the city where my ancestors are buried,'" Neh. 2:4-5 (NLT).* Nehemiah replied to the king asking for permission to travel to his home city to rebuild it. But, Nehemiah had already formulated a plan in his head if granted permission to go. Nehemiah knew he had to travel across the treacherous land as well as lacked the provisions to build the wall around the city. Therefore, he was prepared to respond to the king.

Do you have a plan prior to asking God for your breakthrough, someone else's breakthrough, or anything else? And as part of your plan, do you know how long it will take to accomplish it? Well, Nehemiah had methodically calculated his stay! Basically, "all things considered!" *"The king, with the queen sitting beside him, asked, 'How long will you be gone? When will you return?' After I told him how long I would be gone, the king agreed to my request,"* *Neh. 2:6 (NLT).* If you are a husband or a wife reading this, this is a good place to open your *faith bag,* because you need to put this *BIG nugget* in it. I am not sure if you honed in on this,

but the scripture said, *"The king, with the queen sitting beside him…"* Awesome! According to *Amos 3:3 (NLT)--- Can two people walk together without agreeing on the direction?* They made the decision *together*, they were *unified—the power of one.* Remember this because it is a key factor in a successful marriage. Off track, no! Important and insightful revelations such as this, is a lifesaver, relationship builder, and marriage changer. That should have built your faith in and by itself. Nevertheless! Now, back to you.

Well, *Nehemiah's faith* has come your way! 52 days of faith without coming off the wall will give you the results you are looking to achieve!

God put in my spirit to start a project that I wanted to achieve to validate *Nehemiah's faith* in my life before I give this book to anyone else. Therefore, steps were taken to apply *Nehemiah's faith.* The overall desire was to get rid of the "baby fat" around the waistline. Now, it's been some years since being a baby, therefore this had been a lifelong project, even while serving in the military (26 years).

Establishing an abs' workout and applying *Nehemiah's faith* for a persistent 52 days was the challenge. Coming off the wall was not an option. *"But when Sanballat, Tobiah, and Geshem the Arab heard of our plan, they scoffed contemptuously. 'What are you doing?'" Nehemiah 2:19 (NLT).* All previous distractions that had taken precedence were no longer the focus. My *Sanballat, Tobiah, and Geshem* had to wait, which can be other than people.

For example, Distraction No. 1-- not making it to the gym for some reason or other. Therefore, I stopped the workout routine. But, I could have easily completed an abs' workout at home! Distraction No. 2-- stopped due to waiting on a gym partner, No. 3-- stopped because the weather was a deterrent, No. 4-- stopped as a result of lack of time, No.5-- as a result of burnout—basically using the distractions as excuses! How many have you used in your quest for success? Therefore, at some point, I had (you have) to stop the madness and stay in *Nehemiah's faith* for 52 straight days. At the 52dy mark, I could see the results. "Some time later" is a catchphrase I use to relay a point... *meaning after a span of time change can and will take place.*

Faith worked for Nehemiah in his circumstance and it worked for me. And the results of the 52 days *Nehemiah's faith* challenge was dropping from 40-in waist size to a 36-in waist. And continued to a point the *"six pack"* was close in view. The principle works!

However, there were some key factors involved in the 52 days: *perseverance, persistence, consistency, focus, determination, commitment, avoidance, balance, strong leadership, obedience,* and *knowing that a great work was in progress.* Not once have you read it was going to be easy and you will not! Of course, it is not easy! Here is a biblical truth; faith without works is dead. *"In the same way, faith by itself, if it is not accompanied by action, is dead" James 2:17 (NIV).*

What else can you learn from Nehemiah's 52 days faith journey? You will learn that a wall around an entire city can be built in 52 days. You will learn the enemy will show up and distractions will surface when you start a *great work.*

Depending on the project you set out to accomplish and those you include on your team, you will have some setbacks and complaints. *"When I heard their complaints, I was very angry" Nehemiah 5:6 (NLT).* The complaints were coming from the people on Nehemiah's team.

Note: Opposition will come from within as well as from the outside.

Look at the complaints that were distractions to Nehemiah's team members:

1. Other people causing stress upon them: Fellow Jews

2. The wealthy excelling and they were not

3. Food Issues: Lack of food

4. Family Issues: Large families

5. Taxes

6. Mortgages: fields, vineyards, and homes

7. Having to sell children into slavery (Money Issues)

8. Being helpless to fix their personal issues (Money Issues)

9. Lack of money in general

Please take a few nuggets from this section, as well.

There will be people on your team that have similar issues in their lives. But, remember you have a goal to accomplish and the very same distractions could hinder your 52 days project. Point in case, how will you handle your team member's issues, to ensure your mission can be accomplished on time? *"After thinking it over..."* *"Then I called a public meeting to deal with the problem" Nehemiah 5:7 (NLT).* You too must think it over and come up with a plan. I repeat; a plan! As part of your plan you can call a meeting to talk with your team members, so you can get *"a firm grip"* on each problem area. In a similar fashion, these same type people can be those supporting you to accomplish your personal goals: weight loss, song/book writing, spiritual breakthrough, addiction, etc. The purposefully selected people to help you break procrastination habits are the very ones complaining and slowing down your progress.

You can learn from Nehemiah's 52 days faith journey, the very project his team was working on was the one that helped them all overcome in the end. Could it be your next project is writing a new book, which could possibly be the very key that opens a door financially to help those who support you? But, if team members (supporting cast) *"keep adding fuel to the fire,"* you will not be successful in accomplishing your goal or project and neither will they in assisting you to get there. This is the very thing Nehemiah was going through.

Here is another example, if your project is to help people get out of debt, it is not conducive for them to purchase new cars, houses, or furniture when you are putting measures in place to cut cost, pay-off credit cards, and build credit *for them*. As the project manager (*like Nehemiah*), you must communicate with the creditors on behalf of your clients, to let the creditors know what you are trying to accomplish. And if you investigate the interest rates your clients are being charged, you may find they are excessively high.

Remember, this is a faith walk as well, some occasional prayer and fasting are needed to challenge and reason with the authorities coming against your clients. This is important to ensure your clients are successful in the end, even if it means cutting back on how they previously lived. And during this phase times may be hard momentarily. Hopefully, they will allow the plan to work in their favor and at the end of 52 days they too will be able to *"see the forest, not the trees!"*

A similar scenario occurred with Nehemiah's team members. Let me provide clarity. Sanballat, Tobiah, and Geshem (The Creditors) could come in at any time and take what they wanted because the walls were down. The people of Judah did not have any security. And the creditors, for example, were having a field day because they were getting all of the so called *"interest."* Today, many unbelievers, as well as believers' walls, **are down and the enemy is running rampant in their lives.**

One thing I need to point out, remember I said Nehemiah worked for the king in another city? But, he heard about what had happened to his hometown and wanted to fix the problem. Meaning, Nehemiah was away and something negative had occurred in his city. I want you to know, people still lived in the city: **Judah**, but they were not doing anything about it. The people had become *comfortable* and *complacent* in their current condition and the so-called creditors: the likes of Sanballat, Tobiah, and Geshem took advantage of them. It was necessary for the wall to go up. And the walls must go up in your life as well!

Nehemiah presented a plan, received permission, and promised to be back at a certain time. He met all of his milestones once he was able to get the team onboard with the 52dy vision (i.e., project) because he had made a promise to the king and queen to be back at his post at a certain time. You must build your wall in 52 days, then get back to your post, as promised.

The *52 days principle* can be a personal endeavor or a teambuilding project. Nonetheless, if used you should receive the results you set out to accomplish. Even if you do not see the result in its entirety, you will see *change* and the result will be not far in the future. Go home identify a problem, jot down some bullets that will help you correct the problem, then come back to it and develop a detailed plan. Once you derive a plan present it to God and ask Him to help you accomplished it in 52 days, as well as give you faith like that of Nehemiah to accomplish it. *"For I say, through the grace given unto me, to every man that is among you,* *not to think **of** himself more highly than he ought to think; but to*

think soberly, according as God hath dealt to every man

*the **measure of faith**" Romans 12:3 (KJV).*

Try it. It works! Bless you!

Life Change Questions

What does this segment mean to you?

_____

_____

_____

_____

_____

_____

_____

What are you going to do about it?

_____

_____

_____

_____

_____

_____

_____

How are you going to apply it to your life?

_____

_____

_____

_____

_____

_____

_____

NOTES

SEGMENT II
CENTURION'S FAITH
"Authoritative Principle"

It is exciting to explore the next title of faith, the *Centurion's faith*.

This type of faith works from an authoritative perspective. Meaning,

recognizing the authority of a spiritual leader in your presence, but

not only that, also recognizing the authority you possess as a Child

of God; *"taking charge of your destiny!"* Before diving deeper into

this segment a few areas need to be expounded upon 1) a

"Centurion" is identified in certain translations of the Bible as a

"Roman Officer," 2) A Roman Officer is in the Roman military, and

3) Military personnel understand that order and authority exists

within their organization. It is necessary for me to explain this for

those who may not have any military experience or background.

Nonetheless, this segment will teach you how to apply *Centurion's*

faith.

As you grow in understanding of *Centurion's faith* or as the facts

are presented from the Word of God, which provides revelation, you

will have a clearer understanding of how to apply this type faith to your daily life. Again, principles are extracted from the Word of God, which were the *"substance of faith"* that worked in the lives of those who exercised them in the Bible.

First, it is important you recognize the Centurion had a problem that needed a solution. Do you have a problem that needs solving? Now the question is, what are you going to do about it? You may respond and say, I have *already* tried my faith concerning my situation and it did not work! Ok, now let's apply the *Centurion's faith* to the same situation.

Say for instance, you have an existing problem; great, the Centurion had an existing problem as well! *"Lord, my young servant lies in bed, paralyzed and in terrible pain" Matthew 8:6 (NLT).*

Second, the Centurion went to the *"problem solver,"* not just any problem solver; but one who was spiritually connected to God. *"When Jesus returned to Capernaum, a Roman officer came and pleaded with him" Matthew 8:5 (NLT).* Who can you turn to, spiritually, to present your case or pray with you in agreement for a *breakthrough*? Not just anyone, but someone with a strong connection with Jesus Christ!

Certainly not Fortune Tellers, Mediums, Witch Doctors, Enchanters, etc.! It's important to make that clear because there are some people who engage in these types of activities (i.e., spiritual wickedness). I am by no means encouraging or advocating this type of spiritual help. This faith walk is all about Jesus Christ!

What else can you glean from the Centurion? Third, it is important you go to someone who knows they have the power to fulfill your request. All spiritual leaders should possess this power, but all spiritual leaders do not *operate* in this power! Well, Jesus Christ does, at all times, 24/7. He is postured to take on your problem and solve it at a moment's notice. *"Jesus said, 'I will come and heal him'" Matthew 8:7 (NLT).* You too may have a friend or family member in the hospital and need Jesus to come by and heal him.

This is the point where the *Centurion's faith* kicked in action. The Centurion recognized the authority figure in his presence and reflected back on how authority worked in the military. God wants to show you how authority works in His Spiritual Army! But, continue to glean from the Centurion for more insight.

In chapter 8 of Matthew, verse 8 the Centurion said something that is not applicable to people today. *"But the officer said, 'Lord, I am not worthy to have you come into my home. Just say the word from where you are, and my servant will be healed'" (NLT)*. The Centurion did not say **he was not worthy** to come to or advance toward Jesus, which he did. But, he stated he was not worthy for ***Jesus to come to where he lived***, under his roof!

Today, Jesus has *made you worthy* to come to Him and He has opened the door so you can invite Him into your heart, home, situation, or world. *"So then, since we have a great High Priest who has entered heaven, Jesus the Son of God, let us hold firmly to what we believe. This High Priest of ours understands our weaknesses, for he faced all of the same testings we do, yet he did not sin. So let us come boldly to the throne of our gracious God. There we will receive his mercy, and we will find grace to help us when we need it most" Hebrews 4:14-16 (NLT)*. This is the very reason I made the statement that *the Centurion said something that is not applicable to people today.* Are you ready to try Him?

You are probably asking, who gave Jesus this title and authority? Good, you asked because you need to know more about the Higher Authority you can call upon to solve your problem(s). But, feel safe in knowing that ***God*** gave Jesus that title and authority. Jesus did not try to put Himself above God; He followed God's guidance all the way to the cross, to the grave, and to the sky (heaven). Yes, heaven, the place where He sits on the right hand of God making intercession for you.

"Even though Jesus was God's Son, he learned obedience from the things he suffered. In this way, God qualified him as a perfect High Priest, and he became the source of eternal salvation for all those who obey him. And God designated him to be a High Priest in the order of Melchizedek" Hebrews 5:8-10 (NLT). I want you to know that you are safe and secure when you go to Jesus and present your problem(s) to Him, He will begin to fix it in due season because He is *qualified*! Yes, He is the *qualified source of salvation* and *designated* by God just for you!

The Centurion in action! *"I know this because I am **under** the authority of my superior officers, and I have authority **over** my* *soldiers. I only need to say, 'Go,' and they go, or 'Come,' and they come. And if I say to my slaves, 'Do this,' they do it"* Matthew 8:9 *(NLT).* Now, that was a mouth full! Let's put some dynamite under this verse for an explosive experience!

1. He said, "I know…"

2. He said, "I am under authority…"

3. He said, "I have authority…"

4. He said, "I ONLY need to SAY, 'Go,' and they go or 'Come,' and they come

5. He said, "And if I say to my slaves…"

In the simplicity of **authority** and **orders**, there is the underlining action of *spoken words* and *obedience* to those words. Meaning, something has to be *"said"* then an *"action"* should occur in response to the words spoken. For example, if a mother calls her son: "Johnny come here!" The mother spoke; therefore, the son should respond accordingly. You must open your mouth and say something to your problem, situation, etc. You need to find a Bible, then locate scriptures related to your specific situation and repeat them. At that point, you will be saying what God is saying about the problem or situation you are facing. For example, for healing--- *But he was pierced for our transgressions, he was crushed for our iniquities; the punishment that brought us peace was on him, and by his wounds we are healed" Isaiah 53:5 (NIV).* You can replace *we are healed* with *I am healed* and you are on your way to victory.

Remember, the aforementioned scripture from Hebrews 5:8 (NLT) *"Even though Jesus was God's Son, he learned obedience..."* Therefore, your problem, situation, circumstance, issue, etc. must respond to some authority. Meaning, that some spiritual authority (bad or good) has already spoken something over your life, and the very things spoken are manifesting in your life today. And depending on what or who that authority is, either that very same authority or a *HIGHER AUTHORITY* has to make it go away, nothing less.

The Centurion is speaking from a position of authority to a Higher Authority: Jesus Christ. As mentioned previously, the Centurion came to Jesus. Meaning, the lesser authority came to the Higher Authority. How did he know who Jesus was and how did he know the authority Jesus possessed? How did he know that this Jesus could give him the breakthrough that he needed? Look at what the Centurion said, *"I know."* Do you know? Do you know Jesus Christ well enough to go to Him in expectation for a breakthrough in your life? Do you know Him as your High Priest?

The Centurion said, "I am under authority." Do you understand structure and order? Do you recognize that coming to Jesus in faith *"Centurion's faith,"* that the lesser authority attacking you (demonic activity) has to respond to Him "the Higher Authority?" Do you know that in due season when Jesus moves in your situation or against your problem; it is finished? Do you realize that you too possess power to remove situations and problems out of your life? *"Death and life are in the power of the tongue..." (Proverbs 18:21—KJV).*

The Centurion said, *"I have authority."* You too have power! *"I tell you the truth, anyone who believes in me will do the same works I have done, and even greater works, because I am going to be with the Father. You can ask for anything in my name, and I will do it, **so that the Son can bring glory to the Father.** Yes, ask me for anything in my name, and I will do it" John 14:12-14 (NLT)!* This is Jesus speaking in these verses. The scripture reads well, sounds great, and is possible; but you must believe this can be accomplished in Christ's strength and not yours. Ask, Seek, and Knock (ASK)!

When you connect to Jesus, you must *believe* by sowing/planting

this passage of scripture (*John 14:12-14)* into your spiritual garden.

You do this by opening your mouth--speaking (sowing) the seed (the

Word of God), then continue cultivating the seed by repeating and

meditating on it daily (works), waiting in *faith* for a harvest that *will*

manifest. Remember, corn does not grow overnight and neither will

a farmer reap a harvest overnight, but in due time it will manifest.

I must say, if the Higher Authority told you to do it a certain way,

you can take it as a truth and count it done! But, just like the

Centurion, *a man in authority*, it is good that you can recognize

when you need a Higher Authority to move on your behalf. Yes,

sometimes people are not where they should be as children of God,

at a spiritually mature level! But, even the devil knows how to ask

God for things!

Another example is a man named Job. You see, a lesser spiritual

authority "satan" had to go to a Higher Spiritual Authority "God"

for permission to attack Job. Read below:

One day the members of the heavenly court came to present themselves before the LORD, and the Accuser, Satan, came with them. "Where have you come from?" the LORD asked Satan. Satan answered the LORD, "I have been patrolling the earth, watching everything that's going on." Then the LORD asked Satan, "Have you noticed my servant Job? He is the finest man in all the earth. He is blameless—a man of complete integrity. He fears God and stays away from evil." Satan replied to the LORD, "Yes, but Job has good reason to fear God. You have always put a wall of protection around him and his home and his property. You have made him prosper in everything he does. Look how rich he is! But reach out and take away everything he has, and he will surely curse you to your face!" "All right, you may test him"' the LORD said to Satan. "Do whatever you want with everything he possesses, but don't harm him

physically." So Satan left the LORD*'s presence Job 1:*
6-12 (NLT).

Yes, God presented Job to satan, but satan recognized the spiritual coverage around about Job. Therefore, he had to ask for the walls of protection to be removed; then he (satan) could go to work on Job. But, it was not until God: the Higher Authority "removed the wall!"

Remember, do not give in or give up so easily, because *"mustard seed faith"* moves mountains. *"A final word: Be strong in the Lord and in **his mighty power**. Put on all of God's armor so that you will be able to stand firm against all strategies of the devil. For we are not fighting against flesh-and-blood enemies, but against evil rulers and authorities of the unseen world, against mighty powers in this dark world, and against evil spirits in the heavenly places"* Ephesians 6:10-12 (NLT). With God's armor and His wall of protection, the devil cannot harm you. This is where you can sow a seed... *"No weapon that is formed against thee shall prosper; and every tongue that shall rise against thee in judgment thou shalt condemn..." Isaiah 54:17 (KJV).*

The Centurion said a lot of things about what he knew (i.e., I). *"I"* can get you in trouble and *"I"* is probably what got you in the trouble you are currently in.

Have you come to grips with how hierarchical authority works? As a Christian, it is important to understand this type of authority because it causes a change to take place in your life. Once you recognize the people and things coming against you are considered the *lesser authority* to the power of Jesus and even to you who possess the Holy Spirit, you will be able to speak life into dead situations: *"Death and life are in the power of the tongue"*— *Proverbs 18:21 (KJV)* by breaking yokes and chains of bondage, setting captives free, and beginning to live an abundant life as Jesus has already spoken, *"I am come that they might have life, and that they might have it more abundantly" John 10:10 (KJV).*

Have you received any wisdom on how the *authoritative faith principle* works? It was previously mentioned that a principle is *"a law or fact of nature that explains how something works or why something happens."* Therefore, the *Authoritative Principle* is a law or fact that does the same thing and it will work in your life if you allow the Higher Authority to rule in your life; which is Jesus Christ.

It's a trustworthy saying, trusting in Jesus and allowing Him to work in all of your tough situations, you too will get a good report. Look at what He said about the Centurion, *"When Jesus heard this, he was amazed. Turning to those who were following him, he said, "I tell you the truth, I haven't seen faith like this in all Israel" Matthew 8:10 (NLT)! Amaze* is defined as: *to fill with wonder; astound or to show or cause astonishment.*

Do you want to be enlightened for a moment? Then consider this, in the aforementioned paragraphs of this segment a Centurion is identified as a Roman Soldier; well this is what *amazed* Jesus! Please note, the people in Israel are the Jews who were getting the Good News (i.e., the gospel of Jesus Christ), but evidently not *applying* it to their daily lives. Now, here comes a *Roman* who is an outsider, who was not a follower, but only a person that heard about this Jesus and His messages, most likely due to the big stir He was causing. Nonetheless, he had "FAITH to BELIEVE!"

Now, put yourself in the Roman Soldier's shoes! For example, by chance you purchased this book or someone gave it to you as a gift and you really do not have a relationship with Christ or connected to a local church; but nonetheless, you have sense enough to understand the principles behind faith outlined within the book, at some point in your life you take the *unmitigated gall* to use them; that is trusting and having faith without being in the Christian family. You too can amaze Jesus? You can do it! Wouldn't it be awesome for Jesus to say this about *you* to the heavenly host, "I have not seen faith like this in all of... put your *town, city, or state?*" It would be an awesome experience to be there to hear all the awesome testimonies that will come forth as you step out on a renewed faith or a new faith, just by applying the principle of authority!

Therefore, let's settle some things right now because I can sense the question(s) coming. For instance, you may say, what if my situation does not change? How long do I have to wait for my breakthrough? What if my situation gets worse? Listen, your situation will start to change when you start applying the *Authoritative Principle!* God is held accountable and you definitely will not make him a liar. *"God is not a man, so he does not lie. He is not human, so he does not change his mind. Has he ever spoken and failed to act? Has he ever*

promised and not carried it through" Numbers 23:19 (NLT)?

The Bible clearly informs all readers on how the process works, but you must believe and have faith. That is enough to get most people energized and excited to allow Jesus to take action in their lives, I did! Here is a plug-in for all readers, do not *test* God to see if this works, just *trust* Him! Let me provide support, so you will not be misled or misguided, the Word of God says, *"Jesus responded, 'The Scriptures also say, You must not test the LORD your God'" Luke 4:12 (NLT).* Additionally, Deuteronomy 6:16 (NLT) says, *"You must not test the LORD your God..."*

Now, that you have clarity concerning testing God, just apply the faith principle and watch Him work it out. But, if you ever get the nerves to test God, *ONLY* do it according to His instructions. And voilà! Here it is, *"Bring all the tithes into the storehouse so there will be enough food in my Temple. If you do," says the LORD of Heaven's Armies, "I will open the windows of heaven for you. I will pour out a blessing so great you won't have enough room to take it in! Try it! Put me to the test" Malachai 3:10 (KJV)!* You are on your way to a new and better life!

Life Change Questions

What does this segment mean to you?

_____
_____
_____
_____
_____
_____
_____

What are you going to do about it?

_____
_____
_____
_____
_____
_____
_____

How are you going to apply it to your life?

_____
_____
_____
_____
_____
_____
_____

NOTES

SEGMENT III
MUSTARD SEED FAITH
"Diminutive Principle"

In this segment, the *Diminutive Principle* is discussed to ignite your faith. First, let's define *diminutive*: *a word or suffix that indicates that something is **small**.* Why diminutive? Well, I wanted to relate it to the following passages of scriptures:

*"Jesus said, 'How can I describe the Kingdom of God? What story should I use to illustrate it? It is like a mustard seed planted in the ground. It is the **smallest of all seeds**, but it becomes the largest of all garden plants; it grows long branches, and birds can make nests in its shade.'" Jesus used many similar stories and illustrations to teach the people as much as they could understand. In fact, in his public ministry he never taught without using parables; but afterward, when he was alone with his disciples, he explained everything to them" Mark 4:30-34 (NLT).*

In another instance, the mustard seed is used to describe faith, *"'you don't have enough faith,' Jesus told them. 'I tell you the truth, if you had faith even as small as a mustard seed, you could say to this* mountain, *'Move from here to there,' and it would move. Nothing would be impossible"* Matthew 17:20 (NLT). Another amazing scripture! You may not be at that level of Christian maturity or have not given your life to Christ altogether, but just looking at the power of the scripture should motivate you to try your *"mustard seed faith"* concerning your current situations, circumstances, issues, or problems. I want to share another passage of scripture with you that should touch your heart:

Elkanah had two wives, Hannah and Peninnah. Peninnah had children, but Hannah did not. "Why are you crying, Hannah?" Elkanah would ask. "Why aren't you eating? Why be downhearted just because you have no children? You have me—isn't that better than having ten sons?"

Once after a sacrificial meal at Shiloh, Hannah got up and went to pray. Eli the priest was sitting at his customary place beside the entrance of the Tabernacle. Hannah was in deep anguish, crying bitterly as she prayed to the Lord. And she made this vow: "O Lord of Heaven's Armies, if you will look upon my sorrow and answer my prayer and give me a son, then I will give him back to you. He will be yours for his entire lifetime, and as a sign that he has been dedicated to the Lord, his hair will never be cut." As she was praying to the Lord, Eli watched her. Seeing her lips moving but hearing no sound, he thought she had been drinking. "Must you come here drunk?" he demanded. "Throw away your wine!" "Oh no, sir!" she replied. "I haven't been drinking wine or anything stronger. But I am very discouraged, and I was pouring out my heart to the Lord. Don't think I am a wicked woman! For I have been praying out of great anguish and sorrow." "In that case," Eli said, "go in peace! May the God of Israel grant the request you have asked of him." "Oh, thank you, sir!" she exclaimed. Then she went back and began to eat again, and she was no longer sad.

The entire family got up early the next morning and went to worship the Lord once more. Then they returned home to Ramah. When Elkanah slept with Hannah, the Lord remembered her plea, and in due time she gave birth to a son. She named him Samuel, for she said, "I asked the Lord for him." 1 Samuel 1:2, 8-20 (NLT)

The aforementioned may have been quite extensive in explanation, but did it help you?

Let's apply the *diminutive principle* to your situation. Your spiritual outlook toward your small situation may seem *BIG*, the objective here is to apply the principle even though the meaning refers to something small. God wants you to "use it" no matter what! *"Afterward the disciples asked Jesus privately, 'Why couldn't we cast out that demon?' 'You don't have enough faith,' Jesus told them. 'I tell you the truth, if you had faith even as small as a mustard seed, you could say to this mountain, 'Move from here to there,' and it would move. Nothing would be impossible'" Matthew 17:19 -20 (NLT)*. Therefore, just applying these scriptures you will begin to generate results.

Initially, the results may turn out to be small, but at least you have put something in motion; a process has started. Jesus instructed His disciples to apply this principle in their future ministries and they too would see results. But, it is clear the disciples' faith was less than that of a mustard seed: *"You don't have enough faith,"* in which the size of a mustard seed is 1 or 2 mm (0.039 to 0.079 in) in diameter. Looking at the size of a mustard seed, you might wonder if they had any faith at all!

If God has accomplished one thing in your life, which you strongly believe was God and only God, then that is the portion of the mustard seed you need to reflect back on. That accomplishment or portion is your, *"enough!"* It might not make up a whole mustard seed, but it is all you have. It's a start!

Now that you have a starting place, take it to God and tell Him what He did for you in the past and let Him know you have held on to it and strongly believe if He did that one thing for you, He can work out the rest of your issues. And when God shows Himself mighty again in your life, add that to the first event and you will have a half of a mustard seed. It may seem like a slow process, but change is taking place. As you continue to apply the *diminutive principle,* your faith grows from "faith to faith," while simultaneously giving God "glory to glory!"

Jesus did not tell the disciples they needed *mustard tree faith*, no, He started with the smallest part of the plant: "the seed," inadvertently teaching them how to grow a mustard tree type faith. Once you reach the stage of *mustard tree faith*, do not think your reach or expansion is dwarfed. No! Never think your end is near. See, your tree will produce more seeds and start a *"regeneration process."* Now, you can share your faith testimonies with others and they can begin to believe and trust God for themselves; regeneration. You will encourage others through your faith and sow into their lives to a point their breakthroughs will begin to show in the natural; that is called *manifestation.*

Amazingly, only because you took one life event and *believed* it only happened because God intervened on your behalf, which created something **smaller than** a mustard seed for you to build upon. Now you are saying inwardly, *"if God did this for me, surely He can handle what I am going through today!"* At this instance your thoughts might be scurrying around in your head frantically, saying within yourself, what has God done for me? Well, think about this, He woke you up this morning with all of your shortcomings and allowed you to get your hands on this book, just to show you that by applying the *diminutive principle*: *mustard seed faith*, He can surely bring you out of your dead situation. You might say, well, He does that for me every day. And believe it or not, that is a portion of the mustard seed people overlook, ***the small thing***!

Let's not be like the disciples, who walked with, talked with, ate with, slept with, preached with, and healed with Jesus; but yet lacked the faith of a mustard seed. Oh yes, the disciples finally were able to get their acts together! But, God is giving you the knowledge, understanding, and wisdom right now to help alleviate, eliminate, and circumvent the *wilderness experience* in your life. It is an advantage many people do not possess. He is saying to you today, "use it!"

Of course, you want to apply this principle to your life today, but you have reservations about using it and you're skeptical if it will work at all. Therefore, look at what Jesus said to His disciples about the demon in the boy, " *'Lord, have mercy on my son. He has seizures and suffers terribly. He often falls into the fire or into the water. So I brought him to your disciples, but they couldn't heal him.' Jesus said, 'You faithless and corrupt people! How long must I be with you? How long must I put up with you? Bring the boy here to me.' Then Jesus rebuked the demon in the boy, and it left him. From that moment the boy was well" Matthew 17:15-16 (NLT).*

Now, let's take this another step further. *The creator or inventor of a thing knows how that thing operates and how it should function.* In certain circles, people call them the *Original Equipment Manufacturer (OEM).* Therefore, when Jesus would see His creation functioning out of order, He would take an assessment of it to identify where the *malfunction* existed. And when He identified that a person was acting out of character, He knew there was a misfire in the mind, therefore He could easily relate it to a demonic attack.

To further expound, the next step is correcting the malfunction or misfire. In this situation where Jesus cast the demon out of the boy, you see the boy immediately recovered and started functioning properly. Here is another example, *"when Jesus was still some distance away, the man saw him, ran to meet him, and bowed low before him. With a shriek, he screamed, 'Why are you interfering* *with me, Jesus, Son of the Most High God? In the name of God, I beg you, don't torture me!' For Jesus had already said to the spirit, 'Come out of the man, you evil spirit.' Then Jesus demanded, 'What is your name?' And he replied, 'My name is Legion, because there are many of us inside this man.' Then the evil spirits begged him again and again not to send them to some distant place. A crowd soon gathered around Jesus, and they saw the man who had been possessed by the legion of demons. He was sitting there fully clothed and **perfectly sane**, and they were all afraid"* Mark 5:6-10, and 15 (NLT). On many occasions, the disciples missed the revelation of their assignment and the internal power they possessed, but by the grace of God, you will not! As you watch the Creator (Jesus) fix, correct, align, cast out, heal, etc., His creation, all He wants you to do is *emulate* Him! Go back to the New Testament to see why things and people were created the way they are today. Then, learn how Jesus made corrections to His creation.

Picture Jesus creating something or someone and while doing so He makes a mistake *(not going to happen),* but He figures it is too hard to correct, yet He takes the liberty to release it or the person in the earth *"as is."* Can you imagine Jesus "the Higher Authority," "the Creator," "the Omnipotent" being that puzzled He could not correct the flaw or too lazy to start the design over? No! Jesus didn't create anything or anyone with a design flaw! Absolutely not! He could have easily not let it manifest in the earth.

What we consider as ***design flaws*** are things that bring glory unto God! For example, a baby born with no legs, God's focus is not on the baby because He covers the baby; no the focus is on the parents. Meaning, Jesus wants to see if they can love the baby (who represents Him) in the condition he/she is in, just as God loved them (the parents) in the condition they are or were in?

You may ask, where is the author taking me? Basically, the baby did not have a *"Jesus design flaw."* No, the baby was born with a purpose in mind, to see the hearts of the parents.

Jesus created you, but in His sight you do not have any design flaws. He put you here just as you are to see the heart responses of others toward you. *"As Jesus was walking along, he saw a man who had been blind from birth. 'Rabbi,' his disciples asked him, 'why was this man born blind? Was it because of his own sins or his parents'*

sins' 'It was not because of his sins or his parents' sins,' Jesus

answered. **'This happened so the power of God could be seen in**

him. *We must quickly carry out the tasks assigned us by the one who*

sent us. The night is coming, and then no one can work'" John 9:1-

3 (NLT). Christians, and parents alike, should speak life into dead

situations for the power of God to be seen by unbelievers. Why?

Because "there is life in the power of the tongue."

Let's simplify this! Can you trust Jesus enough to ask for your

breakthrough at this moment? If so, say to Jesus, I want to… Now,

put whatever you need to be fixed after the dots! You did it! You

have postured yourself to receive that breakthrough you have been

eagerly and patiently waiting for. Was that too simple for you? Not

enough bells and whistles or booms and bangs for you. Well, let me

take you to the reference.

As Jesus approached Jericho, a blind beggar was sitting beside the road. When he heard the noise of a crowd going past, he asked what was happening. They told him that Jesus the Nazarene was going by. So he began shouting, "Jesus, Son of David, have mercy on me!" "Be quiet!" the people in front yelled at him. But he only shouted louder, "Son of David, have mercy on me!" When Jesus heard him, he stopped and ordered that the man be brought to him. As the man came near, Jesus asked him, "What do you want me to do for you?" **"Lord," he said, "I want to see!"** *And Jesus said,* **"All right, receive your sight! Your faith has healed you."** *Instantly the man could see, and he followed Jesus, praising God. And all who saw it praised God, too. Luke 18:35-43 (NLT)*

Here is the breakdown:

1. A question was asked: *What do you want me to do for you?*

2. A *mustard seed* response was given: *Lord, he said, I want to see!*

3. A breakthrough happened between the two corresponding: *All right, receive your sight! Your faith has healed you.*

Do you see a lot of praying, dramatic falling out and shouting, any abnormal activity or behavior happening? No! Simple right? Obviously, the man did not say he had faith, Jesus said it. The only thing we can take from the man's behavior in this passage of scripture is, *he was tired of being BLIND.*

Jesus is waiting for you, so He can do something simple in your life. The question is are you tired of being blind? Or whatever is going on in your life—are you tired of being tired? It is similar to your car being stuck in mud, you quickly hop out and push the car until it comes unstuck, but there is an enormous problem: mud as far as you can see. And again, you become stuck! Some people keep going down the same road or going in the same direction and continually becoming stuck. Know this, Jesus wants to set you free!

Back to the *diminutive principle*! If, a person watches a car designer long enough, he should pick-up a mustard seed of faith to do at least some, if not all of the things the designer accomplished to design his car. The same principle applies to your observation of the Creator: Jesus, if you study Him enough, you should pick-up at least a mustard seed of faith to move the mountain(s) in your life. Jesus tells you to *"study to shew thyself approved unto God, a workman that needeth not to be ashamed, rightly dividing the word of truth" 2 timothy 2:15 (KJV)*. Then, solidifies it by telling you to *"take my yoke upon you. Let me teach you, because I am humble and gentle at heart, and you will find rest for your souls. For my yoke is easy to bear, and the burden I give you is light" Matthew 11:29-30 (NLT)*.

If, you put all of your problems, situations and circumstances together *(surely they will not be the size of a mountain)*, then apply the *diminutive principle* to your life, you can now sit back and watch your life change for the better. You may say, that's too easy! It is that easy with Jesus, because His requirement is easy, which is to **only** have a *mustard seed of faith*. You may say, "How can I be certain?" Easy response, have mustard seed faith in Jesus and apply the *diminutive principle*, to bring glory to God. In the aforementioned paragraphs of this segment, Jesus is saying to you today through His scriptures, "use it!" Hopefully, today is the start

of the *new you*, because He is a "life changer!"

Life Change Questions

What does this segment mean to you?

_____

_____

_____

_____

_____

_____

_____

What are you going to do about it?

_____

_____

_____

_____

_____

_____

How are you going to apply it to your life?

_____

_____

_____

_____

_____

_____

NOTES

SEGMENT IV
DAVID'S FAITH
"Goliath Principle"

I know, I know! You probably are wondering how did I go from the *Diminutive Principle* (small) to the *Goliath Principle*; something "***big***." Well, at the time David encountered Goliath, he was small in stature, facing a giant. You may feel like you are low on the totem pole of life, but as your faith grows, it now becomes greater than the threat of any Goliath in your life. Remember, mustard seed faith can move mountains!

Can you imagine what a *mustard seed faith* that grows into a *mustard tree* can do in your life?

This segment is inspired by God to strengthen and build your faith at the next level. Because mountain like situations are things or people standing in the way of your progression. These mountains create challenges for you, hindering you from becoming who God really wants you to be; therefore, another level of faith is required. But, having faith like David's *clears the path* for a new *lifestyle*. Meaning, you may need this type of faith when facing a Goliath situation in life, because Goliath can cause physical harm and can actually destroy you!

Can you now grasp how God really wants the best for you? Please do not miss the small details! God is actually exposing the enemy and his tactics to you, while simultaneously revealing spiritual weaponry so you can defeat him. Isn't that awesome.

Later in the book, you will encounter some scriptures you can repeat over and over on your road *"to victory."* Here is some insight on what God wants you to know. He is going to take you places where victory is imminent and you are not going to fight to win the victory. Are you excited yet? You should be! God is working overtime and on time for you. He foreknew you would play the game too long and foreknew you would be down by too many points to win on your own. He is calling a *timeout*, assessing your physical and spiritual condition, and at this point has decided to put in another player; ***"The Goliath Faith Principle!"***

You may say: Why am I being pulled out of the game when I am the one who must use the principle(s)? Well, you are not being pulled out because *"faith without works is dead!"* You must remain in the

game to do your part, but *faith* will do the rest, *"Now faith is the*

substance of things hoped for the evidence of things not seen"

Hebrews 11:1 (KJV). When *faith* is applied, change takes place in

the spiritual realm. It starts in your *mind:* you must believe it *can*

happen (the power of God), which transfer to your faith in action:

you wait in expectation for the manifestation of your breakthrough.

Who wouldn't serve a God like Him; God Almighty?

Now, you are ready to take the plunge into the *Goliath Principle*, so

let's get started! Remember, Goliath can cause physical harm. And

before you apply the *Goliath Principle* you must know your Goliath;

David knew his!

> *Then Goliath, a Philistine champion from Gath,*
>
> *came out of the Philistine ranks to face the forces of*
>
> *Israel. He was over nine feet tall! He wore a bronze*
>
> *helmet, and his bronze coat of mail weighed 125*
>
> *pounds. He also wore bronze leg armor, and he*
>
> *carried a bronze javelin on his shoulder. The shaft of*
>
> *his spear was as heavy and thick as a weaver's beam,*

tipped with an iron spearhead that weighed 15 pounds. His armor bearer walked ahead of him carrying a shield." 1 Samuel 17:4-7 (NLT)

David was the shepherd of his father's sheep, 1 Samuel 17:15 (NLT) *"but David went back and forth so he could help his father with the sheep in Bethlehem."* He was not a warrior like Goliath, *"you're only a boy, and he's been a man of war since his youth" 1 Samuel 17:33 (NLT).* You too may be humble, vulnerable, timid, a free spirit and constantly starring some Goliath in the face: Bully, Abusive Spouse, Abusive Partner, Liar, Deceiver, Backstabber, Authoritative Boss, Evil/Demonic Person, etc. But know that the people of Israel had their Goliath as well, *"as soon as the Israelite army saw him, they began to run away in fright. 'Have you seen the giant?' the men asked. 'He comes out each day to defy Israel. The king has offered a huge reward to anyone who kills him.'" 1 Samuel 17:24-25 (NLT).*

Jesus wants you to know that once you get the *Goliath Principle* in your spirit, the Goliath(s) you are facing will fall. Remember, your Goliath affects other people as well: your children (legacy), wife (helper), friends (supporting cast), co-works (Army), etc. But be assured, Jesus is "King of kings" *Rev. 19:16 (NLT)*. With Jesus, you do not need to fight for a reward. No! A good Soldier fights for others, what's right, and freedoms. Your *"faith"* fights battles before you get to your Goliath; the battle is already won. In a similar fashion, David went to the *place of victory*, not to fight for *victory*. His faith had defeated Goliath before he arrived at *the place of contempt*; it was already in his heart. David had a *"heart after God's own heart."*

I want to develop this portion: ***"a man after his (God's) own heart"*** concerning David's life for you. First, as you read below you will see God talking to Saul, informing him he has been replaced by David. But I want to also show you that even though David was a **boy** and sometime later (as a man) sinned with Bathsheba, **his heart** was **right** toward God before he committed the sin. Look at the next passage of scriptures.

> *But now your kingdom will not endure; the Lord has sought out **a man after his own heart** and appointed him ruler of his people, because you have not kept the Lord's command."*

1 Samuel 13:14 (NIV)

This man was David in *1 Samuel 16:10:13*, who was a **boy** at the time. But, before you read those verses, you should know there were seven other brothers of David's who were presented to God. Now, look at what God says about them.

> *When they arrived, Samuel saw Eliab and thought, 'Surely the Lord's **anointed** stands here before the Lord.' But the Lord said to Samuel, 'Do not consider his appearance or his height, for I have rejected him. The Lord does not look at the things people look at. People look at the outward appearance, but the Lord looks at the heart.'" 1 Samuel 16:6-7 (NIV)*

Now, read *1 Samuel 16:10:13*:

> *Jesse had seven of his sons pass before Samuel, but Samuel said to him, **'The Lord has not chosen these.'** So he asked Jesse, 'Are these all the sons you have?' 'There is still the **youngest**,' Jesse answered. 'He is tending the sheep.' Samuel said, 'Send for him; we will not sit down until he arrives.' So he sent for him and had him brought in. He was*

*glowing with health and had a fine appearance and handsome features. Then the Lord said, **'Rise and anoint him; this is the one.'** So Samuel took the horn of oil and anointed him in the presence of his brothers, and from that day on the Spirit of the Lord came powerfully upon David."*

1 Samuel 16:10-13 (NIV)

The aforementioned scriptures depict David as a *boy*, but he was yet selected/chosen by God to be *king*. I would like to say, please get onboard with Jesus, because *"you are the one"* as well.

I felt the need to explain that to you, because God searches the heart, to see if it is in alignment with His will. When you fall short, a repentant heart is what God looks for. Then, when you do repent (turn away from your sins), God can and will say the same concerning you: *"a man after his own heart."*

Ok, back to the battlefield with David (the boy).

Remember, *giants* fight and defeat *giants*. David may have been small, but he had a giant's (i.e., giant) heart. When your heart is right with God, chains will be broken, walls will fall, demons will flee and Goliaths will be defeated! *"David asked the soldiers standing nearby, 'What will a man get for killing this Philistine and ending his defiance of Israel?'" 1 Samuel 17:26 (NLT).* What will you get when your Goliath falls? Peace, joy, your loved ones, and a fresh start! His, her, or its *defiance* against you will cease.

For the born-again believer, have you ever asked yourself, who is this Goliath coming up against me; a child of the Most High God? Hold tightly to this part of the *Goliath Principle*; because it deals with IDENTIFICATION! First, you must know who you are in Christ Jesus and then ask yourself, "Who or what is this coming up against me?" Take a look at what David said, *"for who is this **uncircumcised** Philistine, that he should defy the armies of the living God?" 1 Samuel 17:26 (KJV).* **Courage in Faith!** You may ask, why is this statement so important when it comes to the *Goliath Principle*? A word of wisdom! *Circumcision* was an outward sign of the covenant between God and His people. Anyone who joined God's people as servants, slaves, etc. went through the same procedure. A male child was circumcised 8 days after birth, which was the guidance God gave to Abraham. In accordance with *Genesis*

17:9-14, God clearly explains this:

> *Then God said to Abraham, "Your responsibility is to obey the terms of the covenant. You and all your descendants have this continual responsibility. This is the covenant that you and your descendants must keep: Each male among you must be circumcised. You must cut off the flesh of your foreskin as a sign of the covenant between me and you. From generation to generation, every male child must be circumcised on the eighth day after his birth. This applies not only to members of your family but also to the servants born in your household and the foreign-born servants whom you have purchased. All must be circumcised. Your bodies will bear the mark of my everlasting covenant. Any male who fails to be circumcised will be cut off from the covenant family for breaking the covenant."*

Therefore, the key points are: circumcision represented a covenant, circumcision represented a relationship with God, and circumcision represented that these were God's people. When David asked the question, *"For who is this uncircumcised Philistine..."* David made a strong statement, while simultaneously highlighting the following facts: the Philistine did not have a covenant with God, but he did; the Philistine did not have a relationship with God, but he did, and Goliath was a Philistine and Philistines were not God's people.

What do you know about your Goliath that will give you the confidence and courage to stand up to him, her, or it? Have you made a covenant with Jesus as your Lord and Savior? What kind of relationship do you have with God? Can God say you are His?

To activate the *Goliath Principle*, you must be persistent, you must know your strengths and weaknesses (for example, if you are good at something have confidence in yourself and know that you are good at doing it), you must be accountable (for example, the very thing you will let go of after completion of this book, partner with someone who will hold you accountable), you have to take responsibility (not just for you, but others), and you must know where your strength comes from (i.e., God). Then you will have a boldness to say, *"for I can do everything through Christ, who gives me strength" Philippians 4:13 (NLT).*

Yes, people will tell you, you cannot do this or that. They will tell you, you will *never* overcome this addiction. They will tell you, you will *never* overcome the burning lust in your body for the opposite or same sex. They may tell you, you will *never* get away from him/her. They may tell you, you have too many bills, or your boss has a grip on you that cannot be broken. And depending on your family, you may have already heard, you will never amount to anything. So sad to hear parents speak death over you or a sibling, because *"there is death in the power of the tongue" Proverbs 18:21 (NLT)* as well as life. These are just a few Goliaths in people lives, but there are many others that are not mentioned and you may have something similar going on in your life, therefore, you may hear or have heard some of the same things along your journey in life.

But, what does the Word of God say about David when he received resistance from people, *"But David persisted. 'I have been taking care of my father's sheep and goats,' he said. "When a lion or a bear comes to steal a lamb from the flock, I go after it with a club and rescue the lamb from its mouth. If the animal turns on me, I catch it by the jaw and club it to death. I have done this to both lions and bears, and I'll do it to this pagan Philistine, too, for he has defied the armies of the living God!* **The Lord** *who rescued me from the claws of the lion and the bear will rescue me from this Philistine'" 1 Samuel 17:34-37 (NLT).*

That was an awesome response. Basically, the takeaway from this is David was the *overseer* of someone else's possessions. He was responsible for someone else's things, but at the same time, these things were a part of his life support as well. Therefore, he would either die defending them or die without them.

Again, to walk in faith like David, you must know God and have a relationship with Him. I want you to really meditate on 1 Samuel 17:38-39 *"Then Saul gave David his own armor—a bronze helmet and a coat of mail. David put it on, strapped the sword over it, and took a step or two to see what it was like, for he had never worn such things before. 'I can't go in these,' he protested to Saul. 'I'm not used to them.' So David took them off again."* Whose armor are you trying to fight in? Are there situations or circumstances you have been trying and trying to succumb, yet your Goliaths are still there?

Could it be you are wearing someone else's gear (no faith)? Or could it be you are wearing the wrong gear, altogether?

It's safe to follow David's example; take it off! David fought wearing God's armor and in the power of God. *"A final word: Be strong in the Lord and in his mighty power. Put on all of God's armor so that you will be able to stand firm against all strategies of the devil" Ephesians 6:10-11 (NLT).* Stop relying on others to do what you can do for yourself! Open your mouth and apply the *Goliath Principle* by saying: I have a covenant with God, I have a relationship with God, I am a child of the Most High God, and DECREE: Who is this uncircumcised Philistine coming against me? Start a personal prayer life and start praying for yourself! God is saying to you today, I am all you need!

Then again, you might not be a born-again Christian and thinking to yourself, how are these principles going to help me? Well, there is good news. Before going any further, let's start by giving you the opportunity to give your life to Jesus Christ my Lord and Savior, and He can be yours too! It is not hard and it does not take all day. The scriptures below are the basic ones used to lead unbelievers to

Jesus Christ and for Him to come into their lives.

> *That if thou shalt confess with thy mouth the Lord*
> *Jesus, and shalt believe in thine heart that God hath*
> *raised him from the dead, thou shalt be saved. For*
> *with the heart man believeth unto righteousness; and*
> *with the mouth confession is made unto salvation.*
> *For the scripture saith, Whosoever believeth on him*
> *shall not be ashamed. For there is no difference*
> *between the Jew and the Greek: for the same Lord*
> *over all is rich unto all that call upon him. For*
> *whosoever shall call upon the name of the Lord shall*
> *be saved. Romans 10:9-13 (KJV)*

If, you have friends who are believers, invite them to be in your presence to witness this awesome experience with you. Ask them to stand with you in faith. Just open your mouth and recite the following out loud to God and He will hear you:

- God forgive me of all the sinful deeds I have done and anything that is not pleasing in Your eyes

- I believe in Jesus Christ as my Lord and Savior

- I believe that He died for my sins

- I believe that You raised Him from the dead, in Jesus' name.

Now that you have done this, allow God to do the rest. I recommend you find a good Bible teaching ministry and inquire about baptism. Ask the leader(s) in the ministry, if there are any classes taught on baptism. If so, make your way to them, then get baptized.

You are on your way once you put all of the aforementioned steps in perspective. Now, let's build you up more in the *Goliath Principle*. What God wants to reveal to you is even though people or things seem larger than life, they have some type of controlling mechanism within them, just as you do. For example, a human who is large in stature has a brain, just as a person who is small. Therefore, if the brain functions are interrupted, the larger person will malfunction and likewise the same will happen to the smaller person. This picture is being painted to provide clarity as it relates to the human size.

Goliath was big in stature and David was small, but they both had brains and if anything interrupts the functioning of their brains, it will cause a malfunction in their activities, capabilities, and mobility. Pay close attention to the following scriptures. When David confronted Goliath, *"he picked up five smooth stones from a stream and put them into his shepherd's bag. Then, armed only with his shepherd's staff and sling, he started across the valley to fight the Philistine"* *1 Samuel 17:26 (NLT)*. The *Goliath Principle* provides a greater provision of spiritual weaponry for you! ***You only need the simple things God has given you to deal with the Goliath in your life.*** You do not need the cold steel and gunpowder or man-made warrior armor to fight your Goliath.

The principle is this: *"take the sword of the Spirit, which is the word of God" (Ephesian 6:17 (NLT)* and use it. By now your *faith bag* should be nearly full, with a plethora of *faith nuggets* to defeat your Goliath.

The Word of God will show and tell you how to defeat your Goliath.

Some people are weighed down with the world's defense mechanisms, where at some point these things can very well be to their demise. Let me clarify this point! There are people who do not know the weapons of God because they do not have a relationship with God. Therefore, they resort to using what they know—cold steel and gunpowder, or some other weapons of destruction.

But, God's *Goliath Principle* teaches something totally different. *"We are human, but we don't wage war as humans do. We use God's mighty weapons, not worldly weapons, to knock down the strongholds of human reasoning and to destroy false arguments. We destroy every proud obstacle that keeps people from knowing God. We capture their rebellious thoughts and teach them to obey Christ. And after you have become fully obedient, we will punish everyone who remains disobedient"* 2 Corinthians 10:3-6 (NLT).

By giving your life to Jesus Christ, you will begin to learn His way and in this instance, begin applying the *Goliath Principle*. And just by being connected with Christ causes you to be victorious! Look at what Jesus is saying to you today, *"take my yoke upon you. Let me teach you, because I am humble and gentle at heart, and you will find rest for your souls. For my yoke is easy to bear, and the burden I give you is light"* *Matthew 11:29-30 (NLT)*. Who wouldn't serve a God like Him; Almighty God? I recommend you pick 5 scriptures (stones) that relate to your situation and go across your **spiritual valley** to fight your Goliath! But, there is more good news for you. Can you just hold on for a few minutes before you head out? I want to show you a few more awesome things about the *Goliath Princ*iple; this will benefit you.

Some people come in possession of awesome words of encouragement from the Bible and even books like this and immediately they takeoff without *strong roots* or a *strong foundation*. In Matthew 13:20-21 (NLT) *"The seed on the rocky soil represents those who hear the message and immediately receive it with joy. But since they don't have deep roots, they don't last long. They fall away as soon as they have problems or are persecuted for believing God's word."* I want you to know the *seed* referred to here is the *Word of God*, which you have encountered through several encouraging scriptures in this book. But, you must

take some time alone and study the Word of God, so it can get in

your spirit. You must find a church that is teaching the Word of

God, so the Word can saturate you and establish deep roots in your

spirit. You must have the Spirit of God, so you can understand all

that awesome Word you are receiving. I do not want you to be

rock soil, but I do want you to have ***deep roots***! As you continue

reading you will receive; ***deep roots***! See, I do not want your

Goliath to shake your foundation after you have received the

Goliath Principles of how to defeat him.

Watch this, *"Goliath walked out toward David with his shield*

bearer ahead of him, sneering in contempt at this ruddy-faced boy.

'Am I a dog,' he roared at David, 'that you come at me with a

stick?' And he cursed David by the names of his gods. 'Come over

here, and I'll give your flesh to the birds and wild animals!'

Goliath yelled" 1 Samuel 17:41-44 (NLT). Have you heard similar

outbursts? I know you have probably heard your Goliath yell at

you. That is the very reason it was necessary for you to hold on for

a few minutes! Yes, this book is exciting, but you must have strong roots and a strong foundation. If not, you too will be like the *rocky soil*. What Goliath just did to David will be a problem or type of persecution to some people and even you, because it portrays: *fear*. And where did this fear come from? Not God, because 2 Timothy 1:7 (KJV) says, *"For God hath not given us the spirit of fear; but of power, and of love, and of a sound mind."*

If your relationship with God is fairly new, shaky, or lacking strong roots, be cautious with your Goliath. Of course, there are numerous believers that have a solid foundation, but depending on their Goliath, they too must approach him with caution. And they too must understand, that as believers; their Goliaths are spiritually driven. For the bible plainly tells the believer, *"finally, my brethren, be strong in the Lord, and in the power of his might… For we are not fighting against flesh-and-blood enemies, but against evil rulers and authorities of the unseen world, against mighty powers in this dark world, and against evil spirits in the heavenly places"* Ephesian 6:10, 12 (NLT).

This may be a lot to take in, but are you tired of your Goliath dominating you? Are you ready to tell your Goliath: timeout? Are you *really* ready to allow Jesus to rule in your life and situation(s)? Then say what David said, read below:

> *David replied to the Philistine, "You come to me with sword, spear, and javelin, but I come to you in the name of the Lord of Heaven's Armies—the God of the armies of Israel, whom you have defied. Today the Lord will conquer you, and I will kill you and cut off your head. And then I will give the dead bodies of your men to the birds and wild animals, and the whole world will know that there is a God in Israel! And everyone assembled here will know that the Lord rescues his people, but not with sword and spear. This is the Lord's battle, and he will give you to us."*
>
> *1 Samuel 17: 45-47 (NLT)*

Long story short, David is saying, God will bring any Goliath who attacks His people down to size; then they can kill him. So, remember giving your life to Jesus makes you God's child and when Goliath defy you, it is as though he is defying God.

For those who are recent converts (i.e., believers), God is now Lord of their lives and his 'Heaven's Armies" are on standby to fight for them as well. And if that is you, you are now on a team with the Lord of Heaven's Armies, your new Spiritual Leader. Therefore, Heaven's Armies are with you and will help fight your battles. Because many times your Goliath comes with a supporting cast, that must be defeated as well.

Life Change Questions

What does this segment mean to you?

_____

_____

_____

_____

_____

_____

_____

What are you going to do about it?

_____

_____

_____

_____

_____

_____

_____

How are you going to apply it to your life?

_____

_____

_____

_____

_____

_____

_____

NOTES

SEGMENT V
ABRAHAM'S FAITH/ELIJAH'S FATE
"Some Time Later Principle"

You have made it this far and it is my hope you are gradually making a decision on which *principle* you will begin to apply to your life. At this stage of the book, it is imperative to reiterate the definition of a **principle**: a moral rule or belief that helps you know what is right and wrong and that influences your actions. The last part stands out, "That influences your actions." But, you have to possess that *belief* that *sometime later* your life can and will change for the better.

Life may have dealt you or a family member a bad hand, but, if you are holding on to God's unchanging hands, the *"some time later principle"* will happen in your life. What or who will influence your action(s)? In this segment, the focus is on the ***"Some Time Later Principle."*** Why does God want you to focus on a period of elapsed time in your life? Well, it is due to complacency or a level of comfort! Actually, He does not want you to drift back into your past, but rather focus on *"the now* and *the future."*

After having received blessings, favor, abundance, prosperity, wealth, healing, restoration, etc. do you still trust God or are you relying on yourself again? Wow! God wants to see where you are in relation to Him! You have been a Christian for some time, maybe years. Life is good! You have a family, house, job, nice things, and attend a good local church. But, do you still have that deep down zeal to trust God no matter what?

Can we talk about Abraham's faith on this journey, to see how serious God is about our relationship with Him? The Bible reveals that *"**some time later**, God tested Abraham's faith. 'Abraham!' God called. 'Yes,' he replied. 'Here I am'" Genesis 22:1 (NLT).* The words *some time later* imply that some time had passed, after God had blessed Abraham. Has God blessed you? Are you focused enough to be tested by God: *some time later?* So, what was the blessing God released into Abraham's life? Well, before Abraham was given his current name, he was called "Abram."

The LORD had said to Abram:

> *Leave your native country, your relatives, and your*
> *father's family, and go to the land that I will show*

you. I will make you into a great nation. I will bless

you and make you famous, and you will be a blessing

to others. I will bless those who bless you and curse

those who treat you with contempt. All the families

on earth will be blessed through you. Genesis 12:1-

3 (NLT)

Has God opened doors like this in your life? Are you a prime

candidate for testing? It was easy for God to do what He said He

would do in Abram's life, but Abram needed to believe that God

could do it. When you received your blessing, did you believe that

God could do it? Did you have a relationship with God at the time,

or even acknowledged it was God? Or after reading this book, will

you believe that God can give you your breakthrough?

The *"some time later principle"* will determine who or what is

influencing your actions toward what God wants you to do. It is a

good principle to apply to your life or current situation. To *believe*

is one thing, but to *do* the hard things God asks of you: *some time*

later is the challenge! What has God allowed you to have, that He could come back and ask for? He gave Abraham something, then came back and asked for it.

Look at Genesis 22:2 (NLT) *"Take your son, your only son—yes, Isaac, whom you love so much—and go to the land of Moriah. Go and sacrifice him as a burnt offering on one of the mountains, which I will show you."* Is your spirit being moved? God wanted Abraham to kill his son! Now, that is a "some time later" experience!

What would you do? Can you reflect back on some conversations, if any, between you and God, concerning what He asked you to do? I would have loved to be present at the time. It would have been like a *"fly on the wall"* experience, being somewhere in the room, taking it all in, but out of sight.

Do you want to know what Abraham did? *"The next morning Abraham got up early. He saddled his donkey and took two of his servants with him, along with his son, Isaac. Then he chopped wood for a fire for a burnt offering and set out for the place God had told him about"* Genesis 22:3 (NLT). Is this a brake stomping moment for you? Pump, pump, & pump! You are probably saying, he actually went? Yes, he did! So, release the brakes so we can continue.

Before you go on, know that *some time later* God actually did the very thing He asked Abraham to do. God sent Jesus in the earth to be the very sacrifice on the cross for you and I. Jesus was His *one and only* Son whom God loved. But, do you know God loved us more? *"For God loved the world so much that he gave his one and only Son, so that everyone who believes in him will not perish but have eternal life. God sent his Son into the world not to judge the world, but to save the world through him" John 3:16-17 (NLT).* Be assured there is something to the: *"some time later principle,"* but continue to read.

Please note that the promise God made to Abram (before his name change) was *progressive* in nature. Take a step back and look at your blessings today. Can you say they were progressive? It takes time for people to achieve certain goals in life or to obtain certain materialistic things. But, who are they giving credit to, God or self? Look how God continued to bless Abram: *"When they arrived in Canaan, Abram traveled through the land as far as Shechem. There he set up camp beside the oak of Moreh. At that time, the area was inhabited by Canaanites. Then the LORD appeared to Abram and said, 'I will give this land to your descendants'" Genesis 12:5-7 (NLT).*

Are you of age, where God has blessed you to leave a legacy to your children, even grandchildren? Has He loaded you down with stuff to a point He can come back and ask for some of it? Are you mature and humble enough to recognize where it all came from? I know there are a lot of questions, but what are your responses?

Did God make this man rich? Yes, He did! I will tell you that: *"Abram was very rich in livestock, silver, and gold" Genesis 13:2 (NLT).* Therefore, what God was getting ready to do in Abram's life was *greater* than what He had already done. God was preparing to take Abram to a *whole new level*! I know, you are thinking, what kind of language is that? Well, there is nothing wrong with being your self sometimes. Watch this, *"the LORD said to Abram, 'Look as far as you can see in every direction—north and south, east and west'" Genesis 13:14 (NLT).*

You are probably thinking, what was this about? It was about God expanding Abram's territory. But, today it is about how God wants to take you to levels unknown to man, just as He did with Abram! He told Abram, *"I am giving all this land, as far as you can see, to you and your descendants as a permanent possession. And I will give you so many descendants that, like the dust of the earth, they cannot be counted" Genesis 13:15-16 (NLT).*

Did God show you how to get what you have today? For Abram to have as much land as he did, he had to do something. He had to take action and apply himself, *"Go and walk through the land in every direction, for I am giving it to you" Genesis 13:17 (NLT).*

God wants to take you to *new levels* in life, but it may require some testing and application. Please do not become complacent with God, because of the few things He has allowed you to have! Know that *"wealth and honor come from you alone (God), for you rule over everything. Power and might are in your hand, and at your discretion people are made great and given strength" 1 Chronicles 29:12 (NLT).* You may know or learned of people who achieved their goals in life and forgot about God. That is if they ever knew

Him! They stopped going to church, stopped praying like they previously had before, and stopped fellowshipping with other believers. And, in some instances, they started putting themselves above you, friends, family, and associates. You have seen this on TV throughout life, but what about real-life believers: Christians. Humility cannot be overemphasized here! *"But thou shalt remember the LORD thy God: for it is he that giveth thee power to get wealth, that he may establish his covenant which he sware unto thy fathers, as it is this day" Deuteronomy 8:18 (KJV).*

Question? ***Are you ready for a: "some time later" experience with God?*** Or are you too young or too old and satisfied with what you have? You may have heard older people enthusiastically say or quickly response they are too old for anything new at this stage of their lives; that they must leave things up to the younger generation.

Well, have you taken a look at the younger generation lately? Some younger readers may frown at that statement, but I am not suggesting anything negative, I only want to share with those who have come of age (i.e., older readers) that they still have a responsibility to the younger generation. Please understand, God has already laid out a plan for your success, but it must be followed, administered, and applied in your life for it to work. He says to Spiritual Leaders, *"similarly, teach the older women to live in a way that honors God. They must not slander others or be heavy drinkers. Instead, they should teach others what is good. These older women must train the younger women to love their husbands and their children, to live wisely and be pure, to work in their homes, to do good, and to be submissive to their husbands. Then they will not bring shame on the word of God. In the same way, encourage the young men to live wisely. And you yourself must be an example to them by doing good works of every kind" Titus 2:3-7 (NLT).*

To my older people (readers), God does not care about your age when it comes to fulfilling His purpose in and through you! He already knows how old you are, because He gave you those days, months, and years. But, when He calls you to or for a work (purpose), He knows you are at the ripe age to fulfill it. Your past, present and future experiences count. God will give you what you need to accomplish His purpose. He did it for Abram.

When Abram was ninety-nine years old, the LORD

appeared to him and said, "I am El-Shaddai—God Almighty. Serve me faithfully and live a blameless life. I will make a covenant with you, by which I will guarantee to give you countless descendants." At this, Abram fell face down on the ground. Then God said to him, "This is my covenant with you: I will make you the father of a multitude of nations! What's more, I am changing your name. It will no longer be Abram. Instead, you will be called Abraham, for you will be the father of many nations. I will make you extremely fruitful. Your descendants will become many nations, and kings will be among them."

Genesis 17:1-6 (NLT)

Is this inspiring you? Remember, most of the people in our generation do not live to age 99 and at this point of Abram's life God is promising him something greater. If you were not aware, it took Noah 120 years to build the Ark. Noah was not 120 years old. No! He was much older. But, that was the allotted time given him to fulfill God's purpose. So, why have you excluded yourself from the power of God? Do you really think you are too old or young that miracles can't be performed in your life?

The Bible shows that: *some time later* the LORD spoke to Abram in a vision and said to him, *"Do not be afraid Abram, for I will protect you, and your reward will be great"* Genesis 15:1 (NLT). This is God talking to him and confirming a blessing in his life. As previously mentioned, Abram had the cattle, flocks, gold, and silver, but you can see here that God wanted to give him even more. Abram did not understand how this was going to take place when he knew he was old and his wife was just as old. He did not understand because he did not have any children. *"But Abram replied, 'O Sovereign LORD, what good are all your blessings when I don't even have a son?'"* Genesis 15:2 (NLT). Abram and Sarai were at an age where their bodies and sexual intimacy appeared to be dead, they thought their lives were coming to an end, but God was just beginning!

God wants to show Himself strong in your life just as well. You are precious and important to God. God revealed this saying to me many years ago: *"There is something that you have that God needs for His people."* You must identify what that "something" is in your life because it will thrust someone else into his/her spiritual destiny: a husband, a wife, a child, a friend, a co-worker, a brother, a sister, a loved one, or a stranger—you never know! Do not count yourself out yet! Fight, fight, and continue to fight! As stated in the bible, "you must fight the good fight of faith!" *"Fight the good fight for the true faith. Hold tightly to the eternal life to which God has called you, which you have confessed so well before many witnesses"* 1 *Timothy 6:12 (NLT).* Please do not give up on yourself; because your story does not end here, you have a *"some time later"* chapter in your storybook!

Look at the move of God in Abram's life Genesis 15:5- (NLT) *"Then the LORD took Abram outside and said to him, 'Look up into the sky and count the stars if you can. That's how many descendants you will have!'* **And Abram believed the LORD, and the LORD counted him as righteous because of his faith.**"

In all the blessings and promises of God forthcoming to you, remember, you have a responsibility to others who now walk in the same shoes you once wore, yes, I said, once wore. Because at the conclusion of reading this book those shoes will no longer belong to you. Remember, Abram was childless and God saw beyond that, so what is missing in your life that God sees beyond? And when He moves in your life, will you hold on to the instructions found in the Word of God, will you guide your children in the *"Way?" "Jesus answered, 'I am the way and the truth and the life. No one comes to the Father except through me" John 14:6 (NIV)*.

God promised and blessed, yet He made a covenant with Abraham, one that caused Abraham to take on responsibility for his actions. *"Then God said to Abraham, 'Your responsibility is to obey the terms of the covenant. You and all your descendants have this continual responsibility'" Genesis 15:9 (NLT)*. For time's sake, let's not go into the covenant God made with Abraham because your covenant will be different than his. The point is to show that an agreement was made between God and Abraham, even down to his descendants!

All things considered, God has blessed Abram who is now called Abraham. But, we know *"some time later"* God came back to test Abraham. Abraham had to sacrifice his ONLY beloved son, who

God gave him with Sarah. What would you do if God blesses you with something awesome, then *some time later* returns to claim it? Wouldn't it be mind-boggling to know that God is willing to give it to you and later in life want it back?

Church leaders must recognize the same thing, God will give a church hundreds or even thousands of members, but they belong to God! Many times you hear that churches stop having cell group ministries because the senior church leaders felt that the lay ministers were trying to take their members and start their own ministry. Please give me a moment to clarify some things here, because God is guiding.

> *Again, the Kingdom of Heaven can be illustrated by the story of a man going on a long trip. He called together his servants and entrusted his money to them while he was gone. He gave five bags of silver to one, two bags of silver to another, and one bag of silver to the last—dividing it in proportion to their abilities. He then left on his trip Matthew 25:14-15; After a long time their master returned from his trip*

and called them to give an account of how they had

used his money Matthew 25:19; Then the servant

with the one bag of silver came and said, "Master, I

knew you were a harsh man, harvesting crops you

didn't plant and gathering crops you didn't cultivate.

I was afraid I would lose your money, so I hid it in

the earth. Look, here is your money back." But the

master replied, "You wicked and lazy servant! If you

knew I harvested crops I didn't plant and gathered

crops I didn't cultivate, why didn't you deposit my

money in the bank? At least I could have gotten some

interest on it." Matthew 25:24-27 (NLT)

For those that are in church leadership, these few scriptures show that the things or people the Master (God) releases to us are actually still His, they are just on loan to us and we are to be good stewards over those things until the Master (God) returns. If, a person leaves, he has made a *CHOICE* and leaving of his free will. Just know, God will send replacements: *some time later*! Enough on that subject, back to you!

When God speaks to you, will you be *prepared* to respond to His request? Abraham did! In Genesis 22:3-9 (NLT):

1. He took men with him

2. He prepared a donkey to carry them and the supplies

3. He brought wood, fire, and a knife

4. He brought Isaac

5. And he built an altar

Here is a phrase I often use when speaking to the saints of God, *"Preparation before the presentation!" For example, "And Elijah said to Elisha, 'Stay here, for the LORD has told me to go to Bethel.' But Elisha replied, 'As surely as the LORD lives and you yourself live, I will never leave you!' So they went down together to Bethel,"* 2 Kings 2:2 (NLT). Preparing for your presentation (God's purpose for your life) requires staying close to your mentor, to ensure you receive all that you need to be successful. That can be your father, mother, spiritual leader, coach, etc., to assure you, that you are ready to be presented. *"When they came to the other side, Elijah said to*

Elisha, 'Tell me what I can do for you before I am taken away.' And Elisha replied, 'Please let me inherit a double share of your spirit and become your successor.' 'You have asked a difficult thing,' Elijah replied. 'If you see me when I am taken from you, then you will get your request. But if not, then you won't'" 2 Kings 2:9-10 (NLT).

If I take you back to the beginning (1 Kings) your eyes will be open to why Elisha stayed close to his mentor. Go with me!

"He replied again, 'I have zealously served the LORD God Almighty. But the people of Israel have broken their covenant with you, torn down your altars, and killed every one of your prophets. I am the only one left, and now they are trying to kill me, too'" 1 Kings 19:14 (NLT).

I want you to get a little more intimate and serious with this scripture because it reveals the seriousness of God and His purpose through your life. You may be the last now or the outcast, but when you get these principles in your spirit, a shift will take place in your life. *"So those who are last now will be first then, and those who are first will* be last" Matthew 20:16 (NLT).

God is waiting on you to release yourself to Him, then He can turn you life around. It is not in your power to defeat the devil whose attacking you. It is in your *faith* that you believe God can defeat him for you.

Elijah revealed to God why he could not go on fulfilling God's purpose, which is an excuse, to God. *"Then the LORD told him, 'Go back the same way you came, and travel to the wilderness of Damascus. When you arrive there, anoint... and anoint Elisha son of Shaphat from the town of Abel-meholah to replace you as my prophet'" 1 Kings 19:15-16 (NLT).*

Can you see it now? If you do not see the seriousness in God's response I will break it down for you. Basically, God said to Elijah, since you are afraid to continue with my plan and purpose and you think this is about *you*; then you are FIRED! Now, go anoint Elisha to replace you! You would think Elijah is asking God for a break, a period of relief, but God also knows Elijah's current heart condition. He knows Elijah is the one for this particular season and that he is thoroughly equipped to perform the work. God knows the same about you!

Many times people think God has missed it in their lives when He calls them to a greater purpose/work. But, God really does not want to hear the excuses. He looks at the end of a thing before the beginning of it, meaning, He knows the outcome before He assigns you to the mission. And He gives all the provisions for you to be successful. Elijah was afraid of Jezebel's threat, but God already had a plan in place. Look at what He said, *"anyone who escapes from Hazael will be killed by Jehu, and those who escape Jehu will be killed by Elisha! Yet I will preserve 7,000 others in Israel who have never bowed down to Baal or kissed him" 1 Kings 19:17-18 (NLT).* God presented a number to Elijah (7000), meaning, He has 7000 more people in place to do the work Elijah was doing, but it was not their season, it was Elijah's. This is exactly why I want you to get intimate and serious with these scriptures. When God puts you on assignment, there is nothing that can stop you from fulfilling it. You may have some resistance, but the purpose will be fulfilled! God does not care about your age or who is coming up against you. He can give you extended life and remove those stumbling blocks forever.

Therefore, when you say your season is up, God takes it serious and respond accordingly. You must follow through with God's instructions to ***prepare*** someone to replace you. Elijah had too because he surrendered his authority over to the enemy. *"So Elijah went and found Elisha son of Shaphat plowing a field. There were twelve teams of oxen in the field, and Elisha was plowing with the twelfth team. Elijah went over to him and threw his cloak across his shoulders and then walked away. Elisha left the oxen standing there, ran after Elijah, and said to him, 'First let me go and kiss my father and mother good-bye, and then I will go with you!' Elijah replied, 'Go on back, but think about what I have done to you'" 1 Kings 19:19-20 (NLT).*

You may be saying, God has not said anything to me! Why should I prepare? Exactly! At this point, God may not have said anything to you, but when He does, will you then prepare?

Remember, the thing God asked Abraham to do was not an easy

thing! God did not ask him to retrieve a bucket of water and bring it to Him. No, it was to take his beloved son (Isaac) to a designated place and present him as a sacrifice, yet we see Abraham *"preparing."*

As for believers or those desiring to be a part of this Christian team, God may require of you; *some time later.* The *"some time later principle"* focuses on how you will respond to the request. Will you be obedient? Will you prepare? Will you trust God in spite of? Abraham did!

> *Then he tied his son, Isaac, and laid him on the altar on top of the wood. And Abraham picked up the knife to kill his son as a sacrifice. At that moment the angel of the LORD called to him from heaven, "Abraham! Abraham" "Yes," Abraham replied. "Here I am!" "Don't lay a hand on the boy!" the angel said. "Do not hurt him in any way, for now I know that you truly fear God. You have not withheld from me even your son, your only son." Then Abraham looked up and saw a ram caught by its horns in a thicket. So he took the ram*

and sacrificed it as a burnt offering in place of his son.

Abraham named the place Yahweh-Yireh (which means

"the LORD will provide"). To this day, people still use

that name as a proverb: On the mountain of the LORD

it will be provided. Then the angel of the LORD called

again to Abraham from heaven. "This is what the

LORD says: Because you have obeyed me and have not

withheld even your son, your only son, I swear by my

own name that I will certainly bless you. I will multiply

your descendants beyond number, like the stars in the

sky and the sand on the seashore. Your descendants

will conquer the cities of their enemies. And through

your descendants all the nations of the earth will be

blessed—all because you have obeyed me." Genesis

22:9-18 (NLT)

You might be thinking to yourself *"too much information (TMI),"*

but if this is not helping you, there is something seriously going on.

It is amazing how *"some time later"* God will require you to give

up something He once gave you to see how much you have fallen in love with it over being in love with Him. I have heard in time past, people fall in love with the created thing rather than the Creator of the thing. But according to the Bible, *"they traded the truth about God for a lie. So they worshiped and served the things God created instead of the Creator himself, who is worthy of eternal praise! Amen" ROMANS 1:25 (NLT).* I want to encourage you today there is a: *ram in the bush* just for your obedience and response to the call of God. Just remember, *"give all your worries and cares to God, for he cares about you" 1 Peter 5:7 (NLT).*

Life Change Questions

What does this segment mean to you?

_____

_____

_____

_____

_____

_____

_____

What are you going to do about it?

_____

_____

_____

_____

_____

_____

_____

How are you going to apply it to your life?

_____

_____

_____

_____

_____

_____

_____

NOTES

SEGMENT VI
PETER'S FAITH
"The Reputation Principle"

You've made it to this *principle*. Evidently, this is a good read for you. The goal is to not shortchange you in your pursuit of reading and learning about *"faith that works."* Look at the subtitle again. Now, search deep within yourself and ask this question. Do I have a friend with an awesome *"reputation"* in whom I can put my trust, similar to that of Jesus'? I know you are trying, but it is going to be hard. *"It is better to take refuge in the Lord than to trust in people" Psalms 118:8 (NLT).*

There are some friends you can put a level of trust in, a spouse for example, but you can put all your trust in Jesus. Try Him for yourself sometime! There is a saying in the Christian community, "He may not be there when *you* want Him, but He will be there… TIME." If you do not know or never heard this saying, this is a good time to fellowship with a Christian friend who can help you complete it. I hope you have a few friends like this!

As stated in the aforementioned sentences, the goal is not to shortchange you. Therefore, sharing this passage of scripture with you is imperative:

> *This is what the Lord says: "Cursed are those who put their trust in mere humans, who rely on human strength and turn their hearts away from the Lord. They are like stunted shrubs in the desert, with no hope for the future. They will live in the barren wilderness, in an uninhabited salty land. But blessed are those who trust in the Lord and have made the Lord their hope and confidence. They are like trees planted along a riverbank, with roots that reach deep into the water. Such trees are not bothered by the heat or worried by long months of drought. Their leaves stay green, and they never stop producing fruit." Jeremiah 17:5-8 (NLT)*

Don't be troubled, I know you have a friend you can confide in, but if you make Jesus your first priority, He will make you His first priority. He will show you people or put you around people to befriend that have His heart and a heart for you. I wanted to share

the aforementioned passage of scriptures with you because I want to

take you on a journey related to a man named Peter, who is a disciple

of Jesus Christ. He is a strong-willed individual, who leads from the

front.

> *About three o'clock in the morning Jesus came*
> *toward them, walking on the water. When the*
> *disciples saw him walking on the water, they were*
> *terrified. In their fear, they cried out, "It's a ghost!"*
> *But Jesus spoke to them at once. "Don't be afraid,"*
> *he said. "Take courage. I am here!" Then Peter*
> *called to him, "Lord, if it's really you, tell me to come*
> *to you, walking on the water." "Yes, come," Jesus*
> *said. So Peter went over the side of the boat and*
> *walked on the water toward Jesus. But when he saw*
> *the strong wind and the waves, he was terrified and*
> *began to sink. "Save me, Lord!" he shouted. Jesus*
> *immediately reached out and grabbed him. "You*
> *have so little faith," Jesus said. "Why did you doubt*

me?" When they climbed back into the boat, the wind

stopped. Then the disciples worshiped him. "You

really are the Son of God!" they exclaimed."

Matthew 14:25-33 (NLT)

Once again, there is a lot to consider in this passage of scriptures. Nonetheless, let's extract from this passage what will help solidify a person's faith. I am not sure about you, but for me, three o'clock in the morning is very early. And if a person is still awake at this time, especially after a long day's work, his/her mental capacity has diminished. Sometimes Jesus comes to us in the wee hours of the morning to see if we are spiritually alert. It can be in dreams, visions, or angelic.

Those who are believers possess Holy Spirit, He does not sleep; He is extremely alert. He can alert us to a visitation of the Lord, whether in a dream, through a vision, or the presence of an angel. This may not have occurred in your life, therefore pray to God and ask Him to visit you in a similar fashion. Believe it because He wants to! *"No, what you see was predicted long ago by the prophet Joel: 'In the last days,' God says, 'I will pour out my Spirit upon all people. Your sons and daughters will prophesy. Your young men will see visions, and your old men will dream dreams" Acts 2:16-17 (NLT).*

In those days Jesus had a reputation of performing miracles, so walking on water shouldn't have been a surprise to those in His inner-circle. And even today He possesses the same power and authority. Are you unsure of the power Jesus possesses? Are you still a "doubting Thomas, *John 20:24-31 (NLT)*?" Do you need confidence concerning Jesus' reputation? Well, He parted the Red Sea for Moses and the children of Israel. It wasn't necessary for them to walk on it; they walked through it on dry land. And to solidify His power, He raised Lazarus from the dead. Who wouldn't serve a Savior like Him?

What is so BIG in your life that even when Jesus says, trust in Me, seek Me first, you shrink back in *fear*? Has the doubting world swayed your belief to a point you even question who Jesus *really is* or for some, *who they really are* in Christ? If you are a believer, you are now a part of His inner-circle, like the disciples of old? Do you have a so-called friend whose reputation of helping others causes you to doubt or be fearful to trust in him? Jesus' reputation is solid;

there is no reason to doubt it. *"I tell you the truth, until heaven and earth disappear, not even the smallest detail of God's law will disappear until its purpose is achieved" Matthew 5:18 (NLT)*. Did the flame ignite inside of your heart after reading this scripture?

How many friends/associates of yours are continually seeing or experiencing the move of God, but operate in fear, especially in overcoming their small situation(s)? *"It's a ghost!"* Are you one of those who use words similar to that of the disciples, only to *downplay* the power and authority of God as a *counterfeit*? Is the miraculous power of Jesus in your life or your friends' lives just a *ghost* or do you consider it real? Peter's friends were present when Jesus appeared. They saw the same thing Peter saw, but they called it a ghost (a counterfeit).

One important objective of this book is to strengthen your belief and cast out all doubts. Every awesome move of God should cause people to shout for joy and not become fearful, especially the sons and daughters of God! For example, a struggling father who left home on a bus but came home with a car. A car he previously did not have and it was full of groceries, at a time when money was lacking and the food was scarce. In this example, the children probably jumped with joy and excitement at the presence of all the new things that were previously lacking. And seeing them show up at their doorsteps most likely caused them to consider the car and food as blessings.

Now, can you imagine those children becoming reclusive toward their father saying, I think daddy was involved in something wrong (i.e., illegal) to acquire these things, basically doubting his ability? Then later, the children exclaim to the father, "we do not want to ride in THAT car or eat THAT food," after the father worked so hard to acquire it or possibly was blessed with it. And through all the doubt the father even presented the children with proper credentials used to qualify for the new car or presented supporting documentation related to how he was blessed with the other things. Amazing isn't it!

Can you imagine how Jesus feels when people doubt His abilities to care for them? Can you fathom in your mind the feeling of Jesus when people treat Him like the children in the example? You may not be able to pull that picture up in your mind, but any caring person would feel hurt!

The scriptures say, *"but Jesus spoke to them at once" Matthew 14:25-33 (NLT)*. This was done to comfort them, because the disciples were terrified. If you are connected to Christ, you should always be in expectation for awesome moves of God to occur in your life.

In the previous paragraphs, it was recommended that you pray and ask God to reveal wisdom to you, either in dreams, visions or through angelic encounters. There are times people need to hear from God, so He can assure them, "Everything is going to be all right!"

Peter was becoming spiritually mature through trials, failures, and life experiences with Jesus. Look at the statement Peter made, *"Lord, if it's really you, tell me to come to you, walking on the water" Matthew 14:28 (NLT)*. It is imperative to clarify one important aspect of Peter's statement by use of the Word of God. Notice, Jesus quickly responded to Peter's request, *"Yes, come" Matthew 14:29(NLT)*, because Jesus knew who He was according to *Matthew 3:16-17 (NLT)*, *"after his baptism, as Jesus came up out of the water, the heavens were opened and he saw the Spirit of God descending like a dove and settling on him. And a voice from heaven said,* **'This is my dearly loved Son, who brings me great joy.'"**

Can I make a shift here momentarily? For the men reading this book, especially this section, please, please speak positive things into your children's lives. God did in the aforementioned scripture: *"This is my dearly loved Son, who brings me great joy."* You are the one who should be telling your daughter she is beautiful and that you love her. And when the wolves of her generation come out of the woods saying, *"You are beautiful, I love you,"* these words will not be new to her ears. Then, she can reply, *"My father has already encouraged me by telling me I was and still am beautiful and that he loves me; now tell me something I don't know!"* Not in arrogance, but with an inner confidence of knowing whom she is. Why? Because daddy has built her confidence to a point she can say, this is not new to me, I have heard this all my life.

In such situations, you have helped your daughter defeat the devil. And if you missed that opportunity along your journey in life, it is not too late to get it RIGHT! You can speak positive things similar to this into your son's life as well! Jesus came back and redeemed many lost people; including me. Many believers at one point did not hear these encouraging and positive words from their natural fathers. And surely, that once-upon-a-time spiritual father (i.e., the *devil*) did not speak these types of encouraging and positive words into their lives.

Today, if you pay close attention to certain songs, he (the *devil*) is even calling your daughters everything but a child of the Most High God. You may or may not know the words men are using to depict young daughters today, but be assured they are not pleasant and they are being repeated so frequently into some of your daughters' lives, they have accepted them as truth. And looking at many daughters today, they are accepting these names to a point they are allowing men to treat them accordingly. Not all young ladies, but it just depends on the location.

Yes, unbelievers are added in this group, therefore, their spiritual father is *still the devil*. Similarly, unbelievers at one point did not hear these encouraging and positive words from their natural fathers.

And surely, their current spiritual father (i.e., the *devil*) is not speaking these types of encouraging and positive words into their lives. The unbelievers should do everything possible to turn this around in their lives! And it starts by believing in Jesus. Because, any words coming out of satan's mouth is a lie. But, if they elect to stay *unbelievers* and keep the *devil* as their father they should not expect to hear any encouraging words! Here is why! *"For you are the children of your father the devil, and you love to do the evil things he does. He was a murderer from the beginning. He has always hated the truth, because there is no truth in him. When he lies, it is consistent with his character; for he is a liar and the father of lies" John 8:44 (NLT).*

This once-upon-a-time spiritual father (i.e., the *devil*) was the father to many Christians today. They were deceived by him and he caused them to miss it, to be lost, to be broken, and to walk in darkness, but God was faithful and rescued them. He spoke words, they heard them, and they came out of darkness. You can speak words that your children have never heard come from you and they will hear, and even now those very words can be the keys to set them free. Dads remember, "there is life in the power of the tongue." So, shower your now *older* daughter and son with words of love, even if it is simply "I love you!"

I always encourage my little ones in church with this, "Remember, if momma, daddy, grandma, or grandpa does not love you; always remember *JESUS LOVES YOU.*" In your mine, you are probably thinking, "I cannot believe he said such a thing!" Well, I do because many kids do not receive the love they should at home and some parents are not nice or loving. And I deal with this in ministry often.

If by chance one of my little ones (at church) is every succumbed by the ways of the world or are out in the world alone and they are counted worthless by family, at least I would have instilled a lasting word in their hearts: "always remember *JESUS LOVES YOU!*" You may live in a perfect world or maybe in a fantasy world, but life is *real* out there. And the devil is unforgiving.

Look around your local area to see if any children similar to this have grown up and are out on the streets now succumbed by some form of addiction, poverty, homelessness, or a negative spirit. I am sure it would be encouraging at this stage of their lives to know that in spite of the current condition, there is hope and Jesus loves them.

Excuse me for taking you off the path, but God wanted me to share that piece with the men out there, it is never too late to reach back into your children lives! You should find them then tell them you love them, and assure and ensure them you are available for them. You still have time! Now back to Peter.

There are two powerful scriptures that relate to Peter's action: *"'Yes, come,' Jesus said. So Peter went over the side of the boat and walked on the water toward Jesus"* Matthew 14:29-30 (NLT). Jesus has assured you one thing through the word of God, *"My sheep listen to my voice; I know them, and they follow me"* John 5:27(NLT). But, there is a scripture that solidifies this one, *"They won't follow a stranger; they will run from him because they don't know his voice"* John 5:5(NLT).

Once you come out of fear, will you step out on faith? Step out, just on the voice of Jesus, who is now your Lord and Savior? Yes, "He is now your Lord and Savior!" Because, if you are not a believer, after reading this book, you should be encouraged enough to try Jesus! He said, *"My sheep listen to my voice!"*

Are you that person or have you seen in churches when Jesus calls many people through spiritual leaders to step out on faith and trust their lives to Him, but though the call is resounding they hold on to the back of the seats and *do not receive* their breakthroughs, their freedom, their salvation! Amazing!!! They are too concerned about what someone might say if they come forth when Jesus calls. Too often, people come to church bound and leave bound! If that is you, I hope the message within this book sets you free in Christ; He is waiting. He wants you and others to come back home. I am reminded of *Luke 15:11-32: The Parable of the Lost Son.* If you really want to experience what it is like to come back home, back to Jesus, please take time to read these scriptures. Jesus gives an awesome example of what He will do when any person returns back to Him.

You should know that Jesus had a *reputation.* And depending on who was evaluating Jesus' walk and accomplishments, determined how He was viewed. A person seeing and understanding Jesus' purpose viewed Him in a positive light. That person heard and believed Jesus' message(s) then became His disciple. But, remember, Jesus went to the *cross*, meaning, there was a group of people who viewed Him in a negative light! That group of people had the following attributes:

1. They did not want to accept change: *The New Testament*

2. They were selfish

3. They were cowards: *What will the people say if I do not kill Him?*

4. They lived by tradition: *This is the way we have always done it*

5. They could not even see to "believe:" *Jesus performed miracles continually*

6. They lacked spiritual knowledge, understanding, and wisdom of the Bible: *Jesus forthcoming in the Old Testament*

7. They always wanted to be in control

Nevertheless, Jesus' reputation preceded him! Therefore, your belief in the facts presented in the Bible concerning Jesus' reputation is the principle you should apply to any situation or circumstance you encounter in your life. Believe He will call you to *"step out"* on faith, which will be your *walking on water experience*! The *reputation principle* will influence your future actions. Either you believe or not! But, the principle worked for Peter!

It is one thing to hear a "feel good" message, but it is another thing to step out on faith (i.e., take action) after hearing the message. It is like going to an event where the excitement is high, people are roaring, they are having a blast, just ecstatic! But, not too far in the near future, reality sets in. The event is over, now far removed. And now you do not know how to channel the excitement or emotions gained from the event into real life circumstances. It was only an eventful "high!"

This occurs in many people lives in churches, the *"feel good"* message ignited their spirits, emotions, and desires. But, on many occasions, the message fizzes out, due to lack of application or lack of continuous feeding of the Word of God in that area of their lives.

Spiritual Leaders need to continue to build them up until they *"get it!"* Meaning, until they apply the knowledge delivered through the message, until manifestations (i.e., results) are produced, and until their faith is taken to the next level. After seeing the results and their faith strengthened, it is now evident the message has become a part of them. Yes, faith comes by hearing! That is the Word of God: *"So faith comes from hearing, that is, hearing the Good News about Christ"* Romans 10:17 (NLT).

But, many people need a shepherd to guide them through this faith walk, until they can walk on their own. For example, picture a baby holding on to a table or chair and Daddy or Mommy is calling him/her to come. Sure he wants to let go and come, but he recognizes there is the distance (space) between them. The parent eventually encourages him to let go and walk over, awesome; he did it!

Now, some time later the parent is in the kitchen and he is holding on to the same table or chair, the encouragement is not there, Mommy or Daddy is not sitting across from him on the sofa and fear sets in. The baby is stuck due to *fear* and *resists* moving forward; growth is stifled. Compare that to the Christian life.

You just received an awesome "faith message," but you are no longer at church and the Pastor and saints have all gone home. The message lies dormant or sometimes fades away! Point is, do not be one of those people who thrive to hear these types of messages and never apply them to your existing situations or personal goals and desires. It's not about getting excited, but trusting and believing God who is faithful to do what He says He will and can do; *"God is not a man, so he does not lie. He is not human, so he does not change his mind. Has he ever spoken and failed to act? Has he ever promised and not carried it through" Numbers 23:19 (NLT)?*

Now let's go back to when Peter walked on the water and encountered the wind. Here are some important tips about the *"wind:"* *"But when he saw the strong wind and the waves, he was terrified and began to sink" Matthew 14:30 (NLT).* This is important for you to understand, Peter did see something; he saw the effects of the wind. For example, you can stand in the middle of a parking lot and feel the wind blowing, but you will not see it. Then, all of a sudden you see a piece of paper blowing across the parking lot, sand and debris swirling around—at that point you are seeing the effects of the blowing wind. And Peter experienced the same thing. He saw the effects of the wind, even on the water, which were the waves. This troubled him, simultaneously creating *doubt!*

How many people you know are seeing the effects of powerful forces in their lives? The Word of God says we shouldn't fear: *"For God has not given us a spirit of fear and timidity, but of power, love, and self-discipline" 2 Timothy 1:7 (NLT)*. A closer look at *Matthew 14:24 (NLT)* reveals a key nugget: *"Meanwhile, the disciples were in trouble far away from land, for a strong wind had risen, and they were fighting heavy waves."*

This verse is just before the disciple saw Jesus walking on the water. Meaning, Peter already knew there were strong winds and heavy waves. But, in verse 30 when it was time for him to walk on the water, he became fearful of them.

The takeaway from this is, you may already know your current situation exists and it may look bad, but stand on the Word of God when you step out to take control *over it.* Keep the confidence that you are *"in control!"* Why? The situation was already in your life before you got your hands on this book, so there is no reason to fear now. Remember, *"a final word: Be strong in the Lord and in his mighty power" Ephesians 6:10 (NLT).* You are not in this fight alone! The devil is only trying to keep you from receiving your breakthrough. Basically, the devil wants you to *"abort"* the future plan(s) of God in your life! Do not let him do that to you. Jesus wants you to keep your focus on Him. Why let your circumstance, situation, or mess throw you off track now?

You have been looking at and dealing with it far too long and it may have created some fear in your heart, but now that you have a weapon to fight with and a partner to assist; call your situation what it really is "finished!" This is where things get even better. Now you can start helping someone else because you now have the key to correcting, fixing, or eliminating your issues.

Who do you know is sinking, has lost hope, given up, and do not know which way to turn? After reading this book, you just might be the very person to bring him up out of his slump, restore him, or share a word from God that will save him. Yes, trials and tribulations are inevitable, but God's word says... *"Even when I walk through the darkest valley, I will not be afraid, for you are close beside me. Your rod and your staff protect and comfort me,"* Psalm 23:4(NLT), so stay encouraged, start relying on and trusting in Him. His reputation is solid!

Life Change Questions

What does this segment mean to you?

_____

_____

_____

_____

_____

_____

_____

What are you going to do about it?

_____

_____

_____

_____

_____

_____

_____

How are you going to apply it to your life?

_____

_____

_____

_____

_____

_____

_____

NOTES

SEGMENT VII

BLIND FAITH
"The Service Dog Principle"

After much thought and prayer as to what this last segment would be, God revealed the aforementioned topic: Blind Faith. *"For we walk by faith, not by sight"* *2 Corinthians 5:7 (KJV)* is the scripture that sparked this segment. Therefore, if you are not walking in *blind faith*, then you are walking by *natural sight*. Because, *"faith is the substance of things hoped for, the evidence of things not seen"* *Hebrews 11:1 (NLT),* the believers' walk is in the spiritual realm. If, you lose your natural sight, can you still see? No, not naturally!

The principle here is: if you are blind you need assistance. Close your eyes, now start walking—having difficulty, right? Same way spiritually! If you are walking in spiritual blindness, you need spiritual assistance. Use your *spiritual service dog* to take you to where God wants you to go.

Please put this nugget in your faith bag: *"So faith comes from*

hearing, that is, hearing the Good News about Christ" Romans
10:17 (NLT).

The scripture did not say faith comes from seeing therefore you hear
and follow by the guidance of the Word of God and Holy Spirit.

The word *we* in *2 Cor. 5:7* is plural, meaning more than one. But, it
is not just talking about anyone; no it is referring to *believers.* If you
are reading this book and you are not a believer, an open invitation
is extended to you to be in the *"we"* group the scripture is referring
too. Therefore, the verse is saying *we* walk. There is a direction *we*
are going, but to get to that location *we* can only get there by using
one of God's methods.

The first is faith: *braille faith*! You may not know what braille is;
braille is defined as *"a system of raised dots that can be read with
the fingers by people who are blind or who have low vision"*--
Merriam-Webster.com.

In the book of Hebrews, there is a verse, which supports the believer walking in blind faith. The word of God says, *"Now, faith is the substance of things hoped for, the evidence of things not seen"* *Hebrews 11:1 (KJV). It is a basic truth, fact, or belief that braille is a tool used to help the blind move around.* Walking by *faith* and *not by sight* means you are moving from point A to B not by what you see, but what you trust and believe God can/will do!

God has put you on a course or path and released you to feel your way through by running your spiritual hands over the words in the Bible by studying and meditating on the Word of God! Feeling your way through (by trusting in the unseen), it may be hard at times, but the more you practice, the easier it becomes, to the point it becomes second nature.

A naturally blind person must study the connecting dots and remember their formation to know what their meanings are, and this comes with practice. When it is time to recall the meaning(s) of the dots from memory, the blind person quickly does so and reacts accordingly. Basically, being blind causes people to adopt an adjusted lifestyle! And it is the same spiritually as you walk by faith and not by sight because according to the Word of God you must *"study to shew thyself approved unto God, a workman that needeth not to be ashamed, rightly dividing the word of truth" 2 Timothy 2:15 (KJV)*. With braille, you cannot see it—you don't need too, but you can feel it by touch.

God's braille system in *Hebrews 11:1* is *faith*. You must feel it in our hearts! Your faith has to become a passion that hurts when your breakthroughs do not come when you want them, but yet you know they are coming. Having the need for God to a point of hitting rock bottom, but yet holding on to His unchanging hands is an experience many people have encountered. But, you hold on because you know He will come through on time; just not at your timing! That will be the trying of your patience and faith! Can you wait on God? Or are you the one who takes off and tries to fix your own situations?

Can a blind man see?

Yes, Christian blind men and women can see! But, only through or by the methods God uses! What method are you using?

In verses 6 thru 8 of 2 Corinthians you will see while you are here in this dark world using God's methods to see, you are actually separated from Him in the natural/physical sense. But, spiritually, you are connected! *"Therefore we are always confident, knowing that, whilst we are at home in the body, we are absent from the lord: (for we walk by faith, not by sight:) we are confident, I say, and willing rather to be absent from the body, and to be present with the lord" 2 Corinthians 5:6-8 (KJV).*

The scripture states, *"at home!"* When you are "at home" in your natural body, you are still living in the natural earth. But, God is Spirit and in heaven. So there is a separation that has to stay unified to create *oneness.* You must allow Holy Spirit to keep you united. You may ask, how does this occur? Well, one method is in your *worship*: *"For God is Spirit, so those who **worship** him must **worship** in **spirit** and in truth" John 4:24 (NLT).*

The other method is by *faith*: through your conversion from *death* to *life* by giving yourself to Jesus Christ, allowing Him to be Lord and Savior over you. *"But God is so rich in mercy, and he loved us so much, that even though we were dead because of our sins, he gave* *us life when he raised Christ from the dead. (It is only by God's grace that you have been saved!) For he raised us from the dead along with Christ and **seated us with him in the heavenly realms** because we are united with Christ Jesus" Ephesians 2:4-6 (NLT).*

Some people have become *at home* in the earth and in the flesh, to a point once they have completed their assigned purpose in the earth, leaving to go to their rightful home is a challenge. Earth has become their Bahamas, Mexico, Peru, Dubai, or the US Virgin Islands. Can you really repeat verse 8 with confidence and with a true heart: *"we are confident, I say, and willing rather to be absent from the body, and to be present with the lord"*?

Again, the verse is saying *we* walk. This tells you there is a direction believers are to go, but to get to that destination they can *only* get there by using God's second method. God's second method is *the service dog*. Remember, one definition of a principle is a law or fact of nature that explains how something works or why something happens. I hope we can agree that *it is a basic truth, fact, or belief that service dogs help the blind get/move around.*

According to the Americans with disabilities act, "service animals are defined as dogs that are individually trained to do work or perform tasks for people with disabilities." The dog must not be a pet, but be specially trained to assist the handler with something directly related to his or her disability. Emotional support dogs are not considered service animals.

Please do not get stuck on the word *dog* as it is used with the things of God! But, Shepherds do have helpers: *sheepdogs*. But, it is a fact that service animals do work or perform tasks for people with disabilities. Many of *people* have disabilities, which are more spiritual than physical, in churches than in the world, believers than unbelievers, or vice versa. An explanation will be provided, so please do not put a wall up that will keep you from receiving your breakthrough.

Your spiritual service dog is **Holy Spirit** (this is a *like as* principle as an example). He may not be trained like the natural service dog, but He is in tune with the Almighty God. *"But, it was to us that God* *revealed these things by his Spirit. For his Spirit searches out everything and shows us God's deep secrets" 1 Corinthians 2:10 (NLT).* He is so in tune that he knows your *disabilities* (e.g., addictions, sexual immoralities, filthy communication "cursing," lying, alternative lifestyle, stealing, jealousies, unforgiveness, etc.) and knows exactly what to do to *assist* you to overcome and get to where God wants you to be. *"But in fact, it is best for you that I go away, because if I don't, the Advocate (Comforter) won't come. If I do go away, then I will send him to you" John 16:7 (NLT).* Can a blind man see? In Christ, yes he can and so can you!!! *"We walk by faith, not by sight!"* Holy Spirit is not your pet either, but He is your Comforter, He is there to assist you!

> *And I will ask the Father, and he will give you another Advocate, who will never leave you. He is the Holy Spirit, who leads into all truth. The world cannot receive him, because it isn't looking for him and doesn't recognize him. But you know him, because he lives with you now and later will be in you. No, I will not abandon you as orphans—I will*

come to you. "But when the Father sends the Advocate as my representative—that is, the Holy Spirit—he will teach you everything and will remind you of everything I have told you." John 14:16-18, 26 (NLT)

Are you using your *spiritual service dog* or have you left him home? If, Holy Spirit knows your needs or disabilities, then why won't you let Him help you? You may be wondering why you are not growing, moving up, shifting, or coming out from where you are. Could it be you have spiritual cataracts and cannot see? Holy Spirit is always available to guide you to higher grounds, to help you overcome things you cannot, and to teach you how to care for yourself.

The aforementioned description of the natural service dog tells you he will help the person with whatever is *directly related* to his/her disability. Holy Spirit can and will do just that, but, are you allowing him to work in your life? Are you still walking by natural sight: the things you can see, to get you to where you think you should be?

A good nugget to add to your faith bag is *2 Corinthians 5:9-10 (KJV)* *"So whether we are here in this body or away from this body, our goal is to please him. For we must all stand before Christ to be judged. We will each receive whatever we deserve for the good or evil we have done in this earthly body."*

Is this helping you? The takeaway from this scripture is, people may use their own sight to lead them, but they will be judged according to where their eyes take them.

But, if your spiritual service dog (Holy Spirit) is leading, then judgment has already been rendered, because *The Judge* was leading. And He already knows not to "lead you into temptation." *"And lead us not into temptation, but deliver us from evil: For thine is the kingdom, and the power, and the glory, forever. Amen"* *Matthew 6:13 (NLT)*. Not once was it implied you would not be tempted, but God has your back. *"The temptations in your life are no different from what others experience. And God is faithful. He will not allow the temptation to be more than you can stand. When you are tempted, He will show you a way out so that you can endure" 1 Corinthians 10:13 (NLT).*

Please take the escape door God is showing you, it could be an escape window, those do exist you know? Can a blind man see? Remember, *"we walk by faith, not by sight!"* Using God's methods, yes he can and so can you!!!

Life Change Questions

What does this segment mean to you?

_____

_____

_____

_____

_____

_____

_____

What are you going to do about it?

_____

_____

_____

_____

_____

_____

_____

How are you going to apply it to your life?

_____

_____

_____

_____

_____

_____

_____

NOTES

CONCLUSION

NEHEMIAH'S FAITH (52 days Principle) is this the start of your life changing breakthrough? Have you set your 52 days' goal? Do you believe you can make it happen? Do you believe you can transform: mind, body, and spirit in this time frame? Are 52 days realistic?

Remember, Nehemiah did it in 52 days, so can you. He did not beat a personal best record. No, it was planned, because the king asked Nehemiah how long he would be away. Therefore, Nehemiah had set the completion of his milestone at 52 days.

Set your goals and objectives, do not doubt yourself anymore, move forward and make it happen, seek out awesome supporters (teamwork), and claim what rightfully belongs to you. When you partner with Jesus, you can accomplish anything. Find those scriptures to support your goals, those you can have a personal Bible Study with just you and Jesus. And remind Him, He wrote them, you believe them, now you are in expectation for what He said through them. I am excited with you because your past is over and your future is bright. There is nothing that can STOP you now, only YOU.

CENTURION'S FAITH (Authoritative Principle)--who does not want to take charge of their life? Leaders lead from the front! And that is you. It is *time* to take *charge* of you because the devil has had control long enough.

For example, if someone gives you a deed to a house and upon your arrival, someone else greets you at the door and has the nerve to ask you, "Can I help you?" Open your mouth with the deed in your hand and say, "Yes you can!" You should politely explain to the person you are the new owner and you have come to *TAKE* possession of your property. It is imperative you claim what rightfully belongs to you because the devil really is not smart enough to decipher what is his and what is *predestinated* as yours. He thinks all of it belongs to him! He might present you an old deed, but you must present a *new decree* (deed) to break the old.

Christian brothers and sisters, when God *promised* Abram (Abraham), He promised you. I have heard these words in my lifetime, "You cannot enforce the law, if you do not know the law" or "you have no rights, if you do not know your rights"—Pre-Paid Legal. Get in the Word of God and learn what rightfully belongs to you: healing power, authority to set people free, life more abundantly, a double portion, the blessings of Abraham, the fruit of the Spirit, and much more!

MUSTARD SEED FAITH (Diminutive Principle) though so small it makes monumental/astronomical changes. Why did Jesus choose a mustard seed and not a grain of sand? Well, both are definitely small, but the mustard seed has a life inside of it whereas the grain of sand does not. Jesus wants you to know the little you have can make a monumental change in your life, your family members' lives, and those you encounter daily.

You may say within yourself, I don't have enough! And that is exactly what Jesus knew you would say. Jesus wanted you to see the mustard seed ability among the other larger seeds, like the butter bean, avocado, mango, cherry, etc. He wanted you to know, *"Do not despise small beginnings."*

God needs your response to His word. He just wants you to begin the work, to take a step of faith, to get in motion, to lean forward, to change positions, or just start the new you. In the Bible you will find, *"Do not despise these small beginnings, for the Lord rejoices to see the work begin...."Zechariah 4:10 (NLT)*. And just having that size faith causes a mind change about you, your abilities and capabilities.

Now try to fathom in your mind mustard tree faith, which is much larger than the seed. I think you see the picture! You will go to heights unimaginable. And that is where Jesus wants you to be, where He is. In a dominion—unimaginable! He even helps you throughout the Bible by giving examples of what the Kingdom of Heaven (God) is like.

So remember, if you can think it, it can be! If you can imagine (i.e., image) it, it can come to pass and people will follow; that's vision. If you can hope, faith will push it to the surface (i.e., sub-stance). If you can only believe in the unseen, faith will show you a glimpse of it (i.e., evidence). God wants you to have enough faith, so He can show you just a glimpse of your breakthrough before it is fully manifested, which occurs prior to Him closing the deal in your favor.

Mustard seed faith GIVES victory!

DAVID'S FAITH (Goliath Principle) was childlike. It was immature, innocent, but careless enough to trust the Father, who was the *"author and finisher of his faith."* You too should have a childlike faith; just enough to know it is not fully developed, always growing from faith to faith, but yet reliant on the Father.

You remember jumping from the rooftop into the backyard pool, jumping your bike from high hills, holding on to a moving car while on skates, doing a skateboard grind on a long stair rail, or as a baby petting that mean ole' dog that normally would bite people! Wow, speaking to the giant! That same tenacity exists in you, but it has to be channeled differently, with a different purpose, and a different *Guide*, because, this time you are trying to achieve a different goal and outcome.

And look at David, who did not use the giant's size as a gage to measure by, to determine if the match was even or fair. Jesus wants you to think similar to David, do not try to measure up to your giant, because with Jesus you will always out/oversize him. The situation you are preparing to come out of and put behind you is not in your class anymore and is no match for you as a child of God. That situation/circumstance is an uncircumcised, unprotected, unarmored, *existence* that is not covered by God nor is it in a relationship with God and needs to be banished from your life.

Remember, in this warfare, Big Brother is always watching and ready to step in! Ask God to show you which stones (scriptures) to pick up. You have your *faith bag*, so fill it with what you need to be an overcomer. He might show you five, but you will ONLY need one to win the battle!

ABRAHAM'S FAITH (Some Time Later Principle) manifested promises, blessings, and favor to many generations "some time later." Your "some time later" is in the very near future, which is a *change* for the better. Remember, Jesus who is the author and finisher of your faith is making you promises *(Ref. Hebrews 12:2 KJV),* not this author. God is mighty and faithful.

God made an unfailing covenant with Abraham up to the point He took Ezekiel to a valley where very dry bones laid *(Ref. Ezekiel 37:1-14 NLT)*. Ezekiel was instructed to SPEAK life over and into these bones. This was done so God would remain faithful to Abraham because Abraham was faithful. These very dry bones were those of Israel. Israel was a very disobedient people to a point God displaced them from their homeland and destroyed them in this valley. But, God is a God who tends to His word, either written or spoken *(Ref. Jeremiah 1:12 NLT)*.

You may not be able to count/rely on a man, but truly you can count/rely on God! In the past you may have missed it in life or fallen short, people may have said you will not be anything in life, you are worthless, you are the worst child; but I am here to tell you, there is a "some time later!"

God said, the last will be first and the first will be last… you don't believe me; right? Read this, *"So those who are last now will be first then, and those who are first will be last"* Matthew 20:16 *(NLT)*. And you thought God had forgotten about you. You are headed to the front of the line; get ready!

PETER'S FAITH (The Reputation Principle) was it a "moral rule or belief" that helped him know what was right or wrong and influenced his actions? Or was it a "law or fact of nature" that explained how or why Jesus walked on water? Remember, Peter could not see Jesus, only his silhouette. So, what quickened him to step out of the boat? One, faith! Two, His voice!

See, *"faith comes by hearing and hearing by the word of God" Romans 10:17 (NLT)*. Jesus **spoke** words, Peter heard words… *"Come."* Let's not miss a key truth according to *John 1:1, 14—"In the beginning the Word already existed. The Word was with God, and the Word was God. So the Word became human and made his home among us. He was full of unfailing love and faithfulness. And we have seen his glory, the glory of the Father's one and only Son" NLT.*

Now here is the point, Jesus who is the *Word* spoke *words* to Peter and Peter's faith grew, which caused an action… he stepped out of the boat. Another key takeaway from this, Jesus' sheep knows His voice and will respond. That is why you are with Him, you heard His voice and responded.

Jesus' reputation preceded Him! He could be counted on then and can be counted on now. And you can surely count on Him as well!

Trust Him and see the manifestation of God's glory! Joining Jesus' team affords you PROMISES… *"So be strong and courageous! Do not be afraid and do not panic before them. For the LORD your God will personally go ahead of you. He will neither fail you nor abandon you" Deuteronomy 31:6 (NLT).* God took time to tell the people in the Old Testament this and made sure you knew from the New Testament as well… *"don't love money; be satisfied with what you have. For God has said, 'I will never fail you. I will never abandon you'" Hebrews 13:5 (NLT).*

These are words of comfort. You need to hear encouraging words like this from time-to-time, because God knows and understands there will be challenging times in your life. But, you must constantly be aware He is there for you and when those difficult times arise, share His word with Him and watch Him spring into action... *"even when I walk through the darkest valley, I will not be afraid, for you are close beside me. Your rod and your staff protect and comfort me" Psalms 23:4 (NLT)*. Can you see the simplicity in this?

All Jesus wants to know is your level of understanding concerning *"who He is"* come to fruition. It is like riding a bike. Also, it is like riding a rollercoaster, at any time you can hop on the spiritual rollercoaster and scream out His name, He will put a halt to things going on, to allow Him enough time to respond to what dangers are intruding into your life. Then, He will respond to ensure His child, beloved, friend, redeemed is safe! And that is you.

So, it does not matter how low you get or what time you call, He cares. He will take the wealth of the wicked and release it to the righteous (you). Really, you may say? According to *Proverbs 13:22 (KJV)*—*"A good man leaveth an inheritance to his children's children: and the wealth of the sinner is laid up for the just,"* then He confirms it with another scripture, *"God gives wisdom, knowledge, and joy to those who please him. But if a sinner becomes wealthy, God takes the wealth away and gives it to those who please him" Ecclesiastes 2:26 (NLT).* He will make your crooked path straight again. Stay connected, because you WIN!

BLIND FAITH (The Service Dog Principle) God has means: faith and Holy Spirit to guide you in the direction He wants you to go. Need assistance? Two things need to take place spiritual eye surgery, then a prescription of spiritual lenses. Those spiritual cataracts need to be removed from your eyes, afterwards, God needs to prescribe you some spiritual glasses because in this spiritual walk it takes those things to go beyond what you see in the natural.

You may say this author has lost it! And God knew you would think like this, but He always wants to comfort you through His word... *"When the servant of the man of God got up early the next morning and went outside, there were troops, horses, and chariots everywhere. 'Oh, sir, what will we do now?' the young man cried to Elisha. 'Don't be afraid!' Elisha told him. 'For there are more on our side than on theirs!' Then Elisha prayed, 'O LORD, **open his eyes and let him see**!' The LORD opened the young man's eyes, and when he looked up, he saw that the hillside around Elisha was filled* *with horses and chariots of fire" 2 Kings 6:15-16 (NLT).* The young man was not blind, he saw in the natural: troops, horses, and chariots everywhere.

Elijah prayed, but one key thing stood out in his prayer *"let* him see." There are lots of things God did not *let* you see or will not *let* you see. Why? Many people cannot handle seeing the full picture of life because certain things are a phenomenon, a mystery, or revelation to them. The full picture reveals things: truth, future, power, warnings, outcomes, etc. People will become amazed when they see the fullness of God, they will not be able to wrap their minds around what they see, or will not be able to fathom what God is doing at that given time. And these type encounters will cause them not to act accordingly, but react fearfully, because of their level of *faith.*

You may have never experienced this in your life, but you may have heard something similar. For example, people may have said something was revealed to them in a dream or they heard a voice, then they share it with others; but those they share it with cannot and will not believe such a thing happened or could happen: a phenomenon. They cannot fathom it happening because they are responding from a natural point of view and not spiritually.

Many people could not fathom a car driving without the assistance of a human driver, but today it is happening. Now just imagine (i.e., image) being carried away to Korea from the US in your mind, but the journey is only through pictures and television, all because the distance is too great. But, one day a visionary said and believed he could build a machine to connect the two countries. And today, we have airplanes.

Prayer: *Father God, open the eyes of the reader today so he/she can see spiritually. Let him not be afraid of what he is seeing in the natural because he has joined Your team. And let him know there are many more forces with him spiritually than what is seen in the natural.* In previous segments you have read, faith is *"the evidence of things not seen,"* so have Faith!

The devil tries to keep blinders on you to keep you from seeing the truth. He even inserts earplugs (certain music or teachings), so you cannot hear the truth or build your faith. *"The thief's purpose is to steal and kill and destroy" John 10:10 (NLT).* And God is fed up with it and you should be as well.

Ask God for Holy Spirit then allow Holy Spirit to lead you to places unknown, which are good and wholesome places. Now rip off those heavyweights that are weighing you down! Remove and replace those natural glasses with a pair of spiritual glasses from God. Remove the earplugs as well, then go to Church and hear what God is saying to you about your current situations, circumstances, and your new destiny. Break the cycle that has you down and has trickled down through your family line! And remember, *"it is impossible to please God without faith. Anyone who wants to come to him **must believe that God exists** and that he rewards those who sincerely seek him" Hebrews 11:6 (NLT).* Be free, live free, and stay free! *FAITH* will do that for you. God Bless you forever more. Amen!

www.ingramcontent.com/pod-product-compliance
Lightning Source LLC
Chambersburg PA
CBHW072008040426
42447CB00009B/1535